WHAT CURRENT LAW STUDE

SURTHRIVING LAW SCHO ...)

"I *really* wish I read this while I was applying to law school and as a 1L."

"Someone finally took the time to consolidate advice and wisdom that I can reference beyond my 1L experience."

"Most of the popular law school prep books focus on how to achieve on exams and assignments. I really like that this book explores wellness, which is critical for success not just in academic work but in all aspects of life."

"This is super easy to read, the layout is great, and the 'Bottom Line' sections were fantastic."

"I like the structured advice based on the life cycle of a law student. The bullet points and briefly stated advice is what people want these days in our busy world."

"The post-law school tips and guide is extremely beneficial to read as a 3L about to begin their legal journey."

"Super practical. Actual action items that you can implement in your law school journey and legal career. Advice from practicing lawyers can sometimes seem lofty, empty, out of touch. Not the case here at all!"

"The content of the book seems very genuine and non-judgmental. It seems like you truly have a friend who knows what you are going through and is able to give you the tools to help you get through it and succeed."

"This book provides a refreshing take on adapting to law school in a changing technological and legal landscape."

"It's great to see a disinterested person offering advice, given [that] everyone else in the process of law school has their own set of priorities that may not align with a law student; i.e., admissions wants you to come to the school, firm recruiters want you to go to their firm, etcetera. So, I think it's great to have some frank advice that comes with no strings attached."

"This book has it all! It steps through each of the pieces of the law school journey that are daunting and provides helpful tips and tricks to get through it! It is a manageable read which is incredible because that means you can soak up everything it has to offer amidst all of the casebook readings law students have to juggle. For those who haven't committed to school yet, this book offers a fresh perspective on making the commitment and deciding if law school is for you. For those of us almost through it, the book sheds light on the next steps while encouraging balance and mindfulness throughout the journey."

SURTHRIVING LAW SCHOOL
(AND BEYOND...)

SURTHRIVING LAW SCHOOL (AND BEYOND...)

An essential guide to surviving and thriving on your legal (and life) journey

By W. Adam Hunt
with guest contributors

100% of the proceeds from this book will be donated to SEO Law, a program of Sponsors for Educational Opportunity, Inc., a nonprofit organization dedicated to providing supplemental educational and career support to young people from underserved and underrepresented communities.

Softcover ISBN: 978-1-7371843-0-0 eISBN: 978-1-7371843-5-5

Publisher's Cataloging-in-Publication data

Names: Hunt, William Adam, author.
Title: Surthriving law school (and beyond...) : an essential guide to surviving and thriving on your legal (and life) journey / by W. Adam Hunt with guest contributors.
Description: Includes bibliographical references. | Bainbridge Island, WA: W. Adam Hunt, 2021.
Identifiers: LCCN: 2021910870 ISBN: 978-1-7371843-0-0 (paperback) | 978-1-7371843-5-5 (ebook)
Subjects: LCSH Law--Study and teaching--United States. | Law students--United States--Handbooks, manuals, etc. | Law--Vocational guidance--United States. | BISAC LAW / Legal Education | LAW / Legal Profession | LAW / Essays | SELF-HELP / Motivational & Inspirational
Classification: LCC KF283 .H86 2021 | DDC 340/.07/1173--dc23

AUTHOR'S NOTES

I do not have a financial interest in any product, service, or company discussed in this book. They are recommended based wholly on my personal experience and research.

Please note that internet links, third-party websites, resources and their contents may change. Every effort has been made to validate accuracy at the time of publication, but I am only responsible for the content of my own website, surthrivinglaw.com.

Nothing contained herein is intended or should be considered medical advice. Please consult a qualified health care professional for specific questions about improving your personal health and well-being.

EDITOR'S NOTE:

Guest contributions have been lightly edited for clarity and consistency with permission of the contributors.

SURVIVING

\ SƏR-ˈVĪV \

to endure or live through (an affliction, adversity, misery, etcetera)

THRIVING

\ ˈTHRĪV \[1]

growing or developing vigorously; flourishing

SURTHRIVING

(*THE WORD YOU'VE ENTERED ISN'T IN THE DICTIONARY)

the (at times) nonlinear path from surviving to thriving in your life journey

CONTENTS

PREFACE

My editor said that you would probably want to know more about me and my professional background right up front, so here it goes. I've been a practicing lawyer for over a decade now. After my first year of law school, I worked for the U.S. Department of Justice in Washington, D.C., thinking I would pursue government service after graduating. But as my student loans piled up, I decided to accept an offer the following year to work as a summer associate at a large law firm called Heller Ehrman LLP. That firm would go on to declare bankruptcy during my third year of law school, which was obviously not good news. After going through another round of interviewing my 3L year, I luckily received an offer to join Sullivan & Cromwell LLP (S&C) as a first-year litigation associate in their New York City office. I would later move offices (to S&C's much smaller Southern California outpost in Century City), and firms (to O'Melveny & Myers LLP). After a secondment to Sony Pictures, I went on to join their Legal Compliance department as in-house counsel. That role helped me land my current position as the Director of Regulatory & Trade Compliance at a global entertainment company. It honestly makes me exhausted (not to mention a bit stressed) just writing all of that down!

Like many (if not most) practicing lawyers, I've had my share of challenges to navigate throughout my career, including stress management, time management, and people management. Over the years, more and more people began reaching out to me for guidance and insight about how to navigate many of these same career dilemmas and decisions. The more people that I connected with, the more I began to realize how universal some of these experiences were. I also saw how many people could benefit from getting candid, unbiased advice about these difficult career transitions from someone who has been through it themselves and who is willing to talk about it *all*—the good, the bad, and the ugly. This book is my humble attempt to do just that.

Speaking of challenges, it is impossible to ignore the broader societal conditions in which this book is being published (June 2021). As I write this, we have all been caught in a global pandemic, COVID-19, for well over a year now. Police Officer Derek Chauvin was recently convicted of murdering George Floyd, and racial injustice issues are front and center in America, as is lingering political discord. The pandemic impacts of a "current normal" with lockdowns, quarantines, and social distancing has touched on almost everything, including the places we eat, learn, play, worship, and work. Zooming in on the work front, I've had more than my fair share of Zoom calls over the past fifty-two and counting weeks. But I can't complain, having had the incredible privilege of a job where full-time remote work was possible, unlike the many frontline health care personnel and other essential workers who have sacrificed so much in the past year.

When it comes to law school as an institution, we still don't know how much of the pandemic-related changes are here to stay for good. Nor do we know what things will eventually more closely resemble pre-pandemic practices as vaccinations rise and infections (hopefully) fall. While I might not know exactly what classes or interviewing will look like a few years or even a few months from now, I do know that many people will benefit from the advice shared in the pages that follow. I decided not to wait any longer before sharing this critical guidance that anyone—student, lawyer, or the simply curious—can start using right now. Waiting to get help myself is actually one of the very things that created more stress and anxiety for me in the first place. I also strongly believe that focusing on improving well-being in the legal community and having these discussions is even more necessary while we are all struggling in our own unique ways to deal with the complications of life, school, and work during a pandemic.

With so much cause for concern externally, we simply cannot ignore our own internal needs. As discussed further in the Introduction, there is a very intentional reason that the steps on the front cover don't end with dollar signs. This isn't a guide that's focused on how to make more money from your legal career, although of course the importance of achieving financial stability for your overall well-being cannot be ignored. This guide also isn't guaranteed to help you ace any particular exam or create the perfect course outline. You can find plenty of other books out there for those things. This book is about something much deeper and more fundamental. It's about how to build a solid foundation for yourself, one that will help you **SURVIVE** and **THRIVE**—not just in law school, but in life.

I look forward to being part of your journey.

With gratitude,

Adam

W. Adam Hunt
Bainbridge Island, Washington, USA
adam@surthrivinglaw.com

INTRODUCTION

WHY WRITE THIS BOOK?

Why write this book? It's a good question, and one that I was asked by my former law school advisor before publishing this surthrival guide. I didn't write it to talk you out of going to law school. In fact, most of you reading this are probably in law school, about to start law school, or are already committed to going (side note—if you're still making a decision about going to law school, be sure to read "To Go Or Not To Go To Law School, THAT Is The Question..." in the appendix). So why *did* I write this book? To help you make better decisions—at least better ones than I made when I was in your shoes—and ultimately avoid the unnecessary stress and anxiety that defined my law school experience, and much of my personal and professional life afterwards.

This project started out as a modest series of articles on interviewing that I originally published on LinkedIn. My goal was simply to help others learn from my own experiences of getting a job in "BigLaw." As I connected with more friends, colleagues, and others over the years, I came to realize that there was a greater need for concrete and actionable guidance that goes well beyond applications, grades, exams, and getting a job. I also learned that most of these same principles were relevant to many others in the legal profession, including those not on the BigLaw track.

While there is much talk about challenges that law students—and practicing legal professionals—face in terms of things like their mental and physical health and well-being, I wanted to know what actual tools were already out there. Why *isn't* there more of a concentrated focus on well-being in the legal world? I'm still not sure, but I know that I could have used *much* more help myself along the way for managing the stress and anxiety of finding a job, taking the bar exam, working at a large law firm, and figuring out how to pay off over $200,000 in law school loans. I was also determined to find a way to stop ignoring the things I cared about most. No more skipping workouts, meals, or calls to my loved ones because I just *had* to study or finish "one more thing" at work.

As it turns out, I found that most of the solutions to these fairly universal challenges are actually not complicated. In fact, if you spend enough time searching, you will start to find that most of the advice out there relates to the same ideas and concepts that I explore in this guide. Where my approach differs is that I've combined these general concepts with **specific tips and tools** that I know work because I've used them myself to help make real changes in my life on both a personal and professional level.

To borrow a sports analogy, anyone can tell you that you need to "score points" or "play great defense" to win a ball game. But the best coaches give you the tools that you need to excel. That's why in this guide I have focused on providing strategies *and* actual tools that you can start using today to make your journey through law school—and life—easier to navigate. And since no one ever has enough time, I've kept things short and sweet. I want to make sure that you finish the book so you can get to the most important part—using the tools to live a calmer, happier, and ultimately more rewarding life.

ANCHORING IN MINDFULNESS

Speaking of tools, if there is a single word or concept that's the key to "surthriving" in law school and beyond, I'm fully convinced that it is **mindfulness**. At its core, mindfulness is just paying attention. It's doing things with **intention**—or the opposite of doing things "mindlessly" on autopilot (i.e., *not* paying attention).

All sorts of bad things happen in life when you don't pay attention. Your car can run out of gas if you don't watch the fuel gauge. You can run out of money if you don't pay attention to your bank account. And you can definitely run out of energy if you don't pay attention to the amount of sleep and exercise that you're getting every day.

The problem in law school—and in life—is that there are so many things competing for your time and attention. If you aren't intentional about the choices that you're making, you could very well end up like me: in perpetual motion trying to do everything that grabs your attention and constantly feeling overwhelmed and run-down because it is literally impossible to do it all. When there are so many things demanding your attention and energy in today's world, you have to start with a clearly defined sense of what is most important to you. Otherwise you risk "multi-failing" like I did—failing at many things at the same time—and getting distracted by things that aren't as pressing or as necessary as your other more important priorities.

This guide will help you by focusing on tools that will bring mindfulness to different areas of your life: from your finances to interviewing to relationships and connections. In other words, tools that will help you pay attention to the things that matter most to you. If you put this guide down and never pick it up again, you will still be on the path to surviving and thriving if you remember the importance of mindfulness and find ways to be present and make intentional choices in your life.

ELIMINATING "I JUST… " THINKING

Much of mindfulness teaching is about focusing on—and paying attention to—**the present moment**. This doesn't mean you shouldn't ever make plans for the future. It's more about letting go of whatever has happened in the past, and not spending your time and energy worrying about what's to come. It's this second piece in particular that can really get law students and lawyers in trouble, especially if they start playing what I call the **"I just"** game.

This game begins with thinking that you just need to keep putting everything on hold until you reach a certain milestone. For example: "**I just** need to take the LSAT, and then I can get back to my life." The problem is that as soon as you reach the milestone, a new one quickly takes its place, and then you repeat the cycle. The game then continues in an infinite loop of striving to reach something, getting there, and then replacing the goal with something else. Even for those who do go on to make partner, or achieve other goals (like becoming a judge), they can always find another "I just" statement to make and focus on. It can truly be endless.

Do any of these statements sound familiar? If so, then you may already be playing the game...

- **I just** need to finish my law school applications.
- **I just** need to make it through my 1L year.
- **I just** need to make it on to Law Review.
- **I just** need to get a summer associate position.
- **I just** need to graduate.
- **I just** need to pass the bar.
- **I just** need to get through my first year at the firm.

If you start putting important things like relationships or exercise on hold because you "just" need to do that next thing, they might stay on hold indefinitely. This type of thinking also prevents you from enjoying, appreciating, and being grateful for all of the things that you *do* have right now, and everything that you've already accomplished and achieved.

The way to end the cycle is by making different choices **starting today**. If you don't start making conscious decisions to live life fully in the present *now*, you risk spending the rest of your life chasing after goals and goalposts that keep moving further out. And if you don't have time to prioritize and make time for what matters now, I can assure you from experience that it doesn't get any easier as you go through life adding more and more responsibilities, desires, and life changes to the list, such as getting married, buying a house, or having children. As I recall once reading in a parenting book: "Awareness is the key to change."

HOW TO USE THIS GUIDE

I have been very intentional with how this guide is structured. I start off with the most important and foundational thing: a set of tools called the "surthrival toolbox" that anyone can start using *immediately* regardless of who you are or where you are in your journey. This is where you should begin.

While you *could* spend a bunch of time doing searches online and eventually come up with a list of things for your own toolbox, I've already done it for you—or at least provided you with a head start. I want to save you valuable time and effort by consolidating all of the specific tools that have made a significant difference in my own life and career. The point is to give you a set of tools that you can start using *today* to make impactful improvements in your own life to enhance your overall well-being.

On the subject of saving time, I heard loud and clear from current law students and lawyers that adding any extra reading on top of an often very full workload is a big ask. I have designed this guide with that in mind. Each chapter starts with a brief, easy to digest overview, and concludes with a section called "The Bottom Line" to give you a quick and actionable summary of key points from each chapter. I know that you're busy, and I want to make it as easy as possible for you to quickly get the most relevant, important, and helpful information that meets your needs.

To that end, I have divided this guide into the following sections. Depending on where you are in your journey, you may not need all of them right now. Focus on the parts that are currently most relevant to you, and the rest will always be there for you to refer back to during other stages in your life.

- **Part I (Your Surthrival Toolbox)** is the list of strategies and tools that you can start using immediately in your everyday life. I highly recommend that you start here. *Short on time? Check out the Surthrival Checklist at the end of the section!*
- **Part II (Your Legal Journey Begins)** offers additional insights on surthriving in law school, including guest contributions from current law students.
- **Part III (Let's Get A Job!)** is an interview guide that focuses specifically on strategies to help you survive and thrive while interviewing. *Don't miss the custom worksheets that I've created to help you prepare for acing your interviews!*
- **Part IV (Life After Law School)** contains important advice for key career choices and plans after you have graduated from law school.
- **Part V (BigLaw Partner Perspectives)** includes reflections from a current Deputy Managing Partner of a large law firm office, and a former partner who spent more than thirty years at a Vault Top 10 law firm.
- **Part VI (Beyond BigLaw)** offers insights from guest contributors on clerkships, government service, public interest law, a sole practitioner, and an individual who recently co-founded her own law firm. It also includes the perspective of an entrepreneur and author who graduated with a JD-MBA.

- **Part VII (Life After Law)** serves as a reminder that getting a legal degree does not prevent you from exploring other career paths that you might find more rewarding.
- **Appendix** shares my own candid take on the question of should you go to law school.
- **Additional Resources** contains custom worksheets and templates I created (and have used myself) to help support you on your own legal and life journey.

FINAL (INTRO) THOUGHTS

There's a popular saying that reminds us to focus on the horizon: "it's a marathon, not a sprint." As I have reflected on my own experiences for this project, life has often felt more like a hundred-mile "ultramarathon" (or longer!) and I'm still just on mile one or two. And that's okay. The important thing is that I'm trying my best to move forward and make progress, step by step. That's what you are doing, too, by investing in this guide and finding tools and strategies that work for you.

I truly hope I can help give you clarity, confidence, and courage to face any obstacle. While law school may seem like a huge deal (and it is), if this is a choice that you have already made, don't forget that there are many people who would trade places with you in a heartbeat. Alternatively, if you decide not to pursue a career practicing law (or even go to law school in the first place), this guide will still provide you with tools and insights that will help you wherever life takes you.

I look forward to hearing about your own journey and learning from everyone who has found even more useful tools out there. Please don't hesitate to connect with me via email (adam@surthrivinglaw.com) or on LinkedIn for further support. Finally, know that we are in this together and that I am committed to providing further updates, insights, and guidance to support a community of "surthrivers" on the Surthriving Law website.[2]

Part I

YOUR SURTHRIVAL TOOLBOX

Since the goal of this guide is to give you practical advice, I am starting with the surthrival toolbox: a concrete set of actual things to do, acquire, and use in your everyday life that will help you surthrive. In this section, I explain how and why each of the following areas are absolutely essential to surthriving:

- *Meditating*
- *Budgeting*
- *Habitizing*
- *Organizing & Prioritizing*
- *Networking*
- *Philosophizing*
- *Finding Other Tools*

Surthrival Strategy #1:

MEDITATE

RECOMMENDED TOOLS: **HEADSPACE AND CALM APPS**

Every decision is easier to make with a calm mind and clear head. Meditation helps you take a step back, get focused, and stay centered.

Until I read *10% Happier* by Dan Harris, I always thought that meditation was a little too "out there" for me. In a nutshell, Harris—a former network television news anchor—describes how an "on air" panic attack during a national broadcast led him to embrace mindfulness and a regular meditation practice. Harris originally thought that meditation was a bit too "woo-woo" before giving it a shot himself. After experiencing the benefits, Harris started telling people that meditating made him 10% happier. This helped to destigmatize the topic—after all, who doesn't want to be 10% happier?—and led many people to ask him for more information about meditation, prompting him to write his book (and to later launch an app).

How will meditation help you? Why is it the first tool in the surthrival toolbox? For starters, it is a free and easy thing that you can do literally anywhere to quickly relax, regain focus, and control any feelings of anxiety or of being overwhelmed by the sheer number of things you need to accomplish when there isn't enough time to do all of them. Meditation just involves paying attention to something as simple as your breath.

The scientific evidence[3] demonstrating tangible health benefits from meditation is also growing. Professional sports organizations, including the National Basketball Association, are embracing the performance benefits of mindfulness; in fact, the NBA and WNBA have partnered with the meditation app Headspace.[4] The list of highly successful meditators includes everyone from the founder of Apple, Steve Jobs, and other amazingly successful business leaders like Oprah Winfrey and Arianna Huffington, to championship-winning basketball coach Phil Jackson and players such as LeBron James and Kobe Bryant.[5]

One thing all of these high-performing individuals have dealt with—and overcome—is stress. In my experience, each stage of the legal journey can unfortunately be filled with more than its fair share of stress and anxiety. Stress can accompany everything from exams (LSAT, law school finals, bar exams) to applying to law schools, interviewing for firms or clerkships, getting clients, writing briefs and motions, closing deals, and trying cases in court. And that's just on the career front, without including any significant life events totally unrelated to the practice of law.

Meditation is the first tool for surthriving law school—and life afterwards—because of just how much it can help us better manage any number of stressful situations with grace and resilience. In terms of a tool, this is one that I wish I had learned when I was *much* younger (in fact, my kids are big fans of *Sesame Street*'s "Monster Meditations" which can be found on YouTube).[6] One of the biggest benefits I've seen from my own meditation routine is that with time and practice, I can pay better attention—that is, be more mindful of my thoughts and actions—for **the rest of the day** after meditating. Okay, sometimes not *all* day. But you get the idea.

While my meditation journey started with reading *10% Happier*, I personally use and highly recommend the Headspace app to start your journey. The "basics" course uses simple animations featuring the soothing (for me, at least) voice of co-founder Andy Puddicombe—a former monk turned circus performer turned successful entrepreneur—and you can choose more bite-sized guided meditations of just a few minutes. Puddicombe's book, *The Headspace*

Guide to Meditation and Mindfulness: How Mindfulness Can Change Your Life in Ten Minutes a Day, is another great resource if you are just starting your meditation journey.

While Headspace has been a fantastic tool for me, there are countless other resources out there, including some that I use for a change of pace every now and then. On the app front, Calm is another great option; like Headspace, it also has a free trial period, and, for any parents out there, it has stories that can help kids with bedtime. There are also many simple meditations that you can do without any apps or electronics at all. A quick Google search will reveal lots of different breathing exercises, including ones for beginners that are as short as sixteen seconds.[7] You just need to find one that works for you and get started!

For me, there certainly weren't any immediate or noticeable results after my very first ten-minute meditation, or even after my first week of meditating. But after a month or so of doing daily ten-minute meditations using the Headspace app, it became very noticeable to me on days when I *hadn't* meditated. And while it's something that I try to do every morning without fail (see Chapter 3 on "habitizing"), meditation is great because you can be in the middle of any stressful situation—like the bar exam—and just close your eyes and take four deep breaths in and out to reset, re-center yourself, and get some much-needed headspace.

A quick note about "results": *The legal profession tends to attract a lot of very motivated, high-performing individuals (which probably includes most of you reading this right now) who are used to measuring life in terms of what they accomplish. Mindfulness and the tool of meditation are typically referred to as a "practice" for good reason. Mindfulness truly is something that you need to continue to work on so it will improve your life. But those results take time to fully materialize. In other words, the practice of meditation is not a magic pill where you can take a single dose of a five-, ten-, or twenty-minute meditation and be immediately cured of all stress or anxiety. It's more like a supplement that over time will definitely help lead to a happier and healthier life. One way to think of it is as exercise for your mind, just like your body needs regular physical activity.*

THE BOTTOM LINE: Aside from generally feeling more calm, content, and focused, there is one other important thing to highlight about starting a mindfulness practice. Many (if not all) of the other tools and strategies in this surthrival guide require **awareness** to be fully maximized. A meditation practice is quite literally the practice of paying attention to the present moment; having this as a foundation will help you survive and thrive. While the results of a meditation practice might be difficult to measure, in my experience, it offers broad benefits in many different areas of life from work (more focus), to relationships (more connection), and health (less stress and anxiety).

Surthrival Strategy #2:

BUDGET

RECOMMENDED TOOL: **YOUNEEDABUDGET.COM (YNAB)**

It's never too late to start paying better attention to how and where you're spending your money.

The sooner you start paying attention to how you spend your money—and the debts that you accumulate—the more control you will have over your life. This is particularly true for anyone who is considering taking on significant debt to attend law school. In my case, it was $218,614.77 worth of student loans to attend law school, which required monthly payments of $2,602.40 after I graduated.

My failure to use a budget in law school (or immediately after) is my second biggest regret after not developing a meditation practice sooner—which is probably obvious since it's the second tool in the surthrival toolbox. My attitude as a law student was to just keep taking out loans that I would pay off eventually. I can tell you that my current self isn't super thrilled with the decisions that twenty-five-year-old me made about my financial future.

Think twice*: There are many important considerations besides (or in addition to) published rankings when choosing a law school. I encourage you to fully appreciate that scholarship opportunities, even if from a so-called "lower tier" school in the rankings, can actually give you more flexibility in terms of what jobs you're able to take after graduation. There are simply fewer viable job options (outside of large firms) for paying down massive student loans (like the ones I had) after graduating compared to the job options you'll have if you graduate debt-free or close to debt-free. I highly suggest that you think twice before adopting the same kind of thinking that I did when I was in law school, and to instead consider what scholarship opportunities might be available to you, regardless of the school's ranking.*

Let's turn now to some practical guidance. The best advice I can give you, regardless of your age or financial situation, is to consistently start using a budget **ASAP**. I knew that *having* a budget was important, but I just wasn't ever able to find the right tool I could stick with that would help me manage my finances in a sound way for more than a few months (if that).

Luckily, a few years ago I came across a budgeting tool with a funny (but definitely accurate) name: You Need A Budget, or YNAB for short. YNAB is a very affordable app (currently less than ten bucks a month when you get an annual plan)[8] that has a powerful ability to change your approach to money management. I'm not exaggerating when I say that this one app helped to completely turn around my finances. How? By bringing **mindfulness** to how I was using my money.

The secret to YNAB isn't the software (although the mobile app *is* great), but rather the four rules or principles that provide you with a framework to approaching your finances. In my experience, it's these four principles that truly differentiate YNAB from the many other options out there, and that helped me actually change my whole approach to budgeting.

THE FOUR RULES OF YNAB:[9]

1. Give every dollar a job
2. Embrace your true expenses
3. Roll with the punches
4. Age your money

I think that the single best trick about using YNAB is that it gets you slowly saving money each month for all of the things that you want and need, so that when the car breaks down, or when it's time to buy birthday or holiday presents, you already have a "bucket" of money saved up. This helps you to avoid using your credit cards and thus going further into debt. It's not really different than the old-fashioned way of putting money aside in envelopes, but the app's method sure is a lot more practical and effective.

After giving every dollar a job and filling up each of your buckets/categories for the month, the YNAB app makes it super simple to quickly add expenses while you are spending the money (or shortly after). By helping you be more mindful of where each dollar is going—and having more awareness of how much you have left to spend—YNAB could be a complete game-changer for you, as it was me.

For anyone with a significant other, YNAB also has some great insights around activities such as a couples' monthly budget meeting. While that might not sound like the most fun thing in the world, it's very important to get aligned with your partner on how you are *both* spending money. Meeting my future spouse was the most valuable and life-changing part of my law school experience, but we both maxed out on student loans to attend Northwestern. YNAB was the tool that helped get us on track to finally paying off those loans, buying a house of our own, and generally being much more intentional about what we were doing with our money.

Other examples? *There are plenty of other finance apps out there that can help you with budgeting. Two that I've received great feedback about are Qapital and Mint.*

THE BOTTOM LINE: Don't be like me and wait until *after* law school to figure out how to budget, and don't keep taking out loans that your future self will be stuck trying to manage. Every dollar in student loans you take out now is a dollar (plus interest) that your future self is going to have to pay off. By using a budgeting app like YNAB today, you can start doing your future self a huge favor. After all, the less debt that you accumulate *during* law school means more flexibility and financial freedom that your future self will have in life *after* law school.

Surthrival Strategy #3:

HABITIZE

RECOMMENDED TOOLS: ***ATOMIC HABITS* BOOK AND HABIT TRACKERS**

As the famous quote goes, you are what you repeatedly do. Make sure to build habits that will help you become the kind of person you want to be.

Creating—and sticking to—*positive habits* is a critical step in transitioning from surviving to thriving. In survival mode, you are reactive and doing whatever you can to keep your head above water. To thrive, the next step is to become more proactive and intentional about how you are choosing to spend your time. To bring it back to mindfulness (yes, again!), if you are not **intentional** about forming positive habits you risk **mindlessly** going around making unintentional—and sometimes inexplicable—choices about how you are spending your day, week, month, year, and ultimately your life. As the famous quote often attributed to Aristotle* goes, you are what you repeatedly do.

The book *Atomic Habits: An Easy & Proven Way to Build Good Habits & Break Bad Ones* by James Clear is the single best resource I have found for "habitizing" your life. Okay, so I made up the word "habitizing," but I mean the process of creating a set of healthy habits that will help you surthrive in law school and life afterwards. *Atomic Habits* is filled with many great insights to help you create lasting habits, along with actionable advice for your daily life.

Pro tip: *If the last thing you want to do is sit down and read yet another book, I hear you. For anyone who is in that boat (which is probably most of you reading this right now), I highly recommend giving audio books a shot if you haven't already tried them. You probably have more time than you think you do to listen to a book. Going on a run, walking your dog, standing in lines, and driving pretty much anywhere are all perfect opportunities to fit in another chapter or two. And if you listen with the speed setting at 1.25x or 1.5x, then you can actually get through audio books quite quickly. If you love reading but can't seem to*

* For the intellectually curious, the actual quote comes from writer, historian, and philosopher Will Durant's 1926 work *The Story of Philosophy* in which he describes important principles from Aristotle's seminal work *Nicomachean Ethics.*

find the time, award-winning behavioral scientist and author Katy Milkman actually names this practice of combining tedious tasks with fun ones "temptation bundling."[10]

Going back to that famous quote at the start of this section, the most important part of *Atomic Habits* is how **identity change** is framed as the "North Star" of habit change. In other words, habits are a way of getting to a much deeper question: Are you becoming the type of person that you want to become? It never occurred to me to view habits in this way, but something resonated with me deeply after seeing habits presented through this lens. As Clear puts it, "Ultimately, your habits matter because ... [t]hey are the channel through which you develop your deepest beliefs about yourself. Quite literally, you become your habits."[11]

This means that if you want to be a studious person (i.e., the type of person who gets good grades in law school) then you need to create reliable and dependable study habits. For example, habits like "when I get done with class I will study for two hours." The question of what you actually prioritize studying during those two hours is the focus of Strategy #4 (which is coming up next). If your goal is to become a fit and healthy person, then you can focus on habits that support a healthy lifestyle, such as getting more exercise or adopting a plant-based diet. By building habits that support your desired identity, you will become the type of person that you *want* to become.

A key tool highlighted in *Atomic Habits* is setting very specific "implementation intentions." Why are these intentions important? Because it is very easy to *say,* "I'm going to exercise today" but then never get around to actually doing it—especially during law school! Research[12] shows that you're much more likely to actually *do* what you say you will by being super specific (i.e., setting a **clear intention**) about exactly *when* and *what* you are going to do. You can give this a try right now by setting an implementation intention of your own. Try writing down something simple to start, like: "After I put down this book I am going to go fill up and drink a glass of water."

Another great tool to really start thriving is to add multiple good habits on top of each other, a concept that James Clear calls "habit stacking." The idea is that if you already have a habit that you do every day, such as brushing your teeth, then it's *much* easier to simply "stack" a new habit right on top of it. For example, one habit that I started "stacking" right after I finished reading *Atomic Habits* was adding two minutes of push-ups immediately after my morning meditation—Clear recommends doing any new habit for at least two minutes, but you can always do more if you're up for it. The more habits that you can stack together, the less you'll leave to chance about when you'll actually do something that you have already identified as being important to you.

Like free stuff? *If you don't feel like reading another book (or listening to the audio version), you're in luck! As it turns out, there are a bunch of totally* **free** *resources available on the Atomic Habits website. Thank you, James Clear!*

Before moving on to prioritizing, there's still one more helpful tool to mention: **habit trackers**. Habit trackers are exactly what they sound like—they are a checklist of habits that you tick off each day. Based on my experience of trying to get new habits to actually stick, I have found that it is *very* helpful, if not essential, to use a habit tracker to hold yourself accountable when first starting out.

While there is nothing fancy or magical about habit trackers, they are incredibly effective at helping to build **awareness** of your habits. In the words of author, doctor, and all-around spiritual guru Deepak Chopra: "You can't change what you're not aware of."[13] Similarly in *Atomic Habits*, James Clear says that "we must begin the process of behavior change with awareness"[14] because "if a habit remains mindless, you cannot expect to improve it."[15]

What habit tracker should you use? There's plenty of free ones available if you search online, and you could also just make one yourself. But my favorite habit trackers are the pre-printed ones that come included with many journals and planners these days (see my recommendations in the following chapter). James Clear himself has even gotten in on the action, and now sells The Clear Habit Journal which includes—you guessed it—a very handy habit tracker. At the end of the day, the best habit tracker is the one that you'll actually use. Go find it!

THE BOTTOM LINE: Of all the tools, forming positive habits is the one that I admittedly still struggle with the most on a regular basis. Situational factors like having three kids, a busy job, and various life circumstances don't make things any easier. But I've found that it's absolutely critical to be intentional about building good habits in order to truly thrive. So start now! Write down one new positive habit you will do for at least two minutes a day for the next thirty days—meditating from Strategy #1 counts! For best results, try "stacking" it right after an existing habit that's already part of your daily routine, like brushing your teeth. Before you know it, you will be one step closer to living the life—and having the identity—that you have envisioned for yourself.

Surthrival Strategy #4:

GET ORGANIZED & PRIORITIZE

RECOMMENDED TOOLS: **PRODUCTIVITY PLANNER, SELF JOURNAL**

As noted in the prior section, good habits alone won't solve all of your challenges. Finding tools to help better organize how you manage your time and priorities is absolutely critical to your success in law school and beyond.

Unfortunately, you won't automatically achieve all of your goals with good habits alone. If that was the case, I would have stopped at habitizing in Strategy #3, right? The next step to surthriving is figuring out *what* you need to focus on, and *how long* you need to spend actually doing it. In other words, you need to be organized and mindful of how you are **prioritizing your time**, which is by far your most valuable asset. Priorities change from day to day (sometimes moment to moment), and it's up to you to figure out how to plan your schedule and adjust course as needed. Cue that famous and very appropriate quote on planning: "A failure to plan is planning to fail."

Want examples? *I was hoping you would ask! Let's look at studying. Some of your law classes will have more reading or take longer to outline than others. The same thing goes for life after law school when you might need to juggle multiple cases, deals, and projects, while also balancing the needs of your friends and family, and attending to your health and well-being. In order to survive and thrive, you have to be able to stay organized and constantly prioritize—and re-prioritize—your day, week, month, and year.*

The best tool that I have found for organizing and prioritizing—after lots and *lots* of looking, by the way—is a daily planner. Yep, I'm talking about going super old school and bringing back pen and paper. But before you click on the order button for the first planner you come across online, you should know that all planners are definitely *not* created equal. Trust me: I've learned (through sometimes painful trial and error) that the specific type of planner that you decide to use is actually incredibly important.

After purchasing and trying out more than a dozen of the planners rated highest on Amazon (yes, I have the receipts to prove it!), I have found two that I highly recommend: the Productivity Planner by Intelligent Change and the Self Journal by BestSelf. Both are currently available online for approximately $30 and in my humble opinion, they are well worth the investment.

MY FIRST CHOICE: THE PRODUCTIVITY PLANNER

This planner helped me go from what I like to call **multi-failing** (i.e., failing to do many things well at the same time, more commonly known as "multitasking") to focused **single-tasking**. It's also helpful for the basic but absolutely critical job of clarifying what my actual highest priority is versus having five different top priorities, which usually doesn't work out too well for me—see "multi-failing" above. Like the budgeting tool recommended earlier, much of the power from the Productivity Planner comes from its underlying, research-based philosophy. And yes, a daily planner can totally have a philosophy. Here's how the company describes it:

"By setting yourself a maximum of five tasks a day, completing the most important task first, and working on only one at a time with the help of the Focus Time technique, you will be able to finish the projects you have been procrastinating over, tackle difficult tasks with clarity, and maximize your productivity."[16]

Not too shabby for a planner! To break it down a bit more, every day of the Productivity Planner starts with entering your Most Important Task of the Day (if this was the only thing you did today then you'd be satisfied). You then estimate how many thirty-minute blocks of **undistracted** time (a.k.a., "Focus Time") that you think it will take to accomplish this #MITOTD. Ditto for your Secondary Tasks of Importance (number 2 and number 3 in your priorities) and then any Additional Tasks (number 4 and number 5 in priority on your to-do list). Pretty straightforward, huh?

Perhaps the most important element to this system is focusing on **doing one thing at a time**. You do not move on to the second item on your list until your Most Important Task of the Day is done. Not mostly done. Not partly done. **Totally done**. While it is often easy to say you will do something, seeing a task through to completion can be difficult, and sometimes requires greatly increasing your focus and decreasing distraction.

For me, this means not looking at news updates or checking *any* emails during these thirty-minute blocks of focus time. It also means keeping my non-work electronic devices in another room (embarrassing but true, and maybe something worth trying yourself). For you, it might mean no social media scrolling, messaging friends, or coffee breaks. Whatever your distractions are, be sure to eliminate them to the extent possible. If you're not sure what those things are for you, this is the perfect time to work on being more mindful and aware of what is taking you away from your high-priority tasks as you're trying to do them.

More on focus time: *When I first started using the Productivity Planner, it recommended using the Pomodoro Technique®, created by Francesco Cirillo, who based it off a timer that was in the shape of a tomato—"pomodoro" in Italian. Similar to focus time, the idea is to work for an undistracted or uninterrupted block of time, take a short break, such as five minutes, then repeat. You can find many free and basic "tomato timers" online, and like everything these days, there are many apps available as well. And of course, if you still actually have and use one, a watch works just fine, too.*

One final note on the Productivity Planner: If you're looking for an even easier way to get started, the maker of the Productivity Planner recently introduced a new, cheaper (currently just $15), and even more streamlined version of the product called Productivity Sheets.

RUNNER-UP: THE SELF JOURNAL

Based on my experience, the Self Journal is a strong all-around option. If you are already pretty good (or at least better than me) at prioritizing and are looking for more overall flexibility and assistance with longer-term goal planning, then I would suggest going this route instead of the Productivity Planner.

According to the BestSelf Company (makers of the Self Journal), "this 13-week goal planner, backed by science and success psychology, is designed to optimize your day, tackle your goals, and live a more fulfilled life."[17] In the words of company founder and CEO Cathryn Lavery, the Self Journal is "the tool that will empower you to plan your goals, take consistent action, and make each day count as you walk your own path to your best self."[18] The Self Journal Guidebook outlines the following seven "Philosophies and Principles" for how to accomplish these lofty goals:

1. Craft a roadmap for your life
2. Prioritize your most critical tasks
3. Plan your day before it starts
4. Never feel left behind
5. Tracking & reflection
6. Daily positive psychology
7. Consistency & the 20-mile march

The Self Journal itself is filled with features to help you survive and thrive. I've found the most useful and impactful ones for me are the habit tracker and daily rituals sheet, the daily planner pages, the evening reflections, the thirteen-week bucket list, and the weekly planning and reflection pages. There are also daily "freedom pages" that give space for you to use however you want, which is similar to the helpful "dot grid" feature in The Clear Habit Journal.

Still not sold? *Totally fine by me! As mentioned at the start of this book, I don't get a dime from any of the companies or products recommended in this surthrival guide. You can just as easily go the low-tech or budget route if you want and use a piece of paper and the free template that I've provided in the following pages.*

THE BOTTOM LINE: A daily planner helps bring mindfulness and awareness to how you are spending your most valuable asset—your **time**. Using tools like the Productivity Planner and Self Journal can truly have a huge impact by helping you be much more mindful about how you are spending every moment. One basic goal you can start with *today* is writing down one (and only one) top priority, and actually finishing it before moving on to anything else on your to-do list. You don't even need to spend money on fancy pre-printed journals. You can just pull out a blank piece of printer paper and use (or modify) the template I've provided here and on my website.

DAILY ORGANIZATION TEMPLATE

Visit the Surthriving Law website to download a free copy of this template.

Interested in saving money? Instead of buying a fancy journal or planner, you can always just grab a blank sheet of paper and copy (or modify) the following design that I use every day.

Today's date:______________________

URGENT & IMPORTANT TASK(S)	URGENT & NOT IMPORTANT TASK(S)
IMPORTANT & NOT URGENT TASK(S)	**NOT IMPORTANT & NOT URGENT TASK(S)**
TOMORROW'S TASKS 1. ______ 2. ______ 3. ______ 4. ______ 5. ______ 6. ______	**NOTES**
DAILY GRATITUDE 1. ______ 2. ______ 3. ______	**REFLECTIONS**

Why end with a daily gratitude? *The benefits of a daily gratitude practice (for both physical and mental health) are scientifically proven,*[19] *and the practice is something I've found quite helpful in my own life. I recommend using a planner to incorporate gratitude into your daily routine as suggested in the template. You can also find many gratitude journals online (e.g., the 30-Day Gratitude Journal*[20] *by BestSelf Co., makers of the Self Journal discussed earlier in this chapter).*

Surthrival Strategy #5:

BUILD YOUR NETWORK

RECOMMENDED TOOLS: **LINKEDIN, EMAIL**

More than anything, connecting with others can truly help you achieve your professional goals. Remember that work isn't everything—don't lose sight of the importance of creating lasting, authentic personal relationships.

We are now squarely in the thriving part of the surthrival toolbox. Once you have developed a practice of being more mindful, are monitoring your finances, have built out a set of beneficial habits, and are making sure to prioritize where you spend your time each day, then you can start thinking more about how to better *allocate* some of that time.

Creating strong connections with your peers in law school can have some of the longest-term personal benefits—in my case, finding my life partner! At whatever stage of your legal journey you are in, it's always helpful to connect and continue building strong relationships with practicing legal professionals. In short, **networking** is an extremely important place to invest some of your valuable time, energy, and efforts, as it is truly time well spent.

There are demonstrable health benefits from developing strong relationships[21] and building a sense of connection with others. This can be particularly significant during law school or any other time when you find yourself consumed by work, and possibly withdrawing from maintaining healthy relationships. Outside of improving your overall well-being, there are plenty of professional reasons for building your network as soon as possible; to name just two of these reasons, it helps with your job search and gives the possibility of future business development.

While there are (probably) a million, if not more, articles out there on the importance of networking, many of them miss the mark by describing it purely in transactional terms. They focus on things like "getting five business cards" or "sending ten emails per week." I don't even like the term "networking." I prefer to approach it through a more human lens of "connecting" versus "networking." Whatever you call it, I have found that **quality over quantity** matters most when it comes to building your professional network; that is, the quality of the connection that you are seeking to build with someone always trumps the sheer number of people that you should try to connect with. Think about it in terms of social media "friends" or "followers"—the numbers don't do you any good if you don't have genuine connections with people who will take your call or message you back when you need them.

Similarly, I do *not* recommend that you try to attend each and every social or networking opportunity that you can find. Because your time is valuable, it is important to be mindful of—and intentional about—the professional relationships you are trying to form, and how much time you spend trying to create them. Like most things, you shouldn't "over-index" on networking at the expense of all your other priorities. After all, you do still have to sleep, study, exercise, and have some fun along the way. But you shouldn't totally write off networking opportunities, either. I've found that the best approach has often been finding ways to combine a few of these priorities, or buckets, together.

Combining buckets: *One of my favorite law school activities was playing intramural basketball with my roommate (who happened to play professionally in Europe and could make a shot from pretty much anywhere on the court). It gave me a chance to exercise, connect with law school classmates, and network with people from other graduate programs in the league. I also found that the summer in between my 1L and*

2L year was a perfect time to connect with classmates who I didn't know as well, particularly ones who were spending their 2L summer in the same city as I was. Many of them were totally up for a casual conversation over coffee, lunch, or cocktails—I just had to ask!

Once you are actually "in front" of someone at an event (in-person or virtually), the best place to start is to engage them with **authentic interest and curiosity**. This is true whether you are at law school orientation, a recruiting event, or just a casual cocktail hour. Same thing goes regardless of whether you are talking to the managing partner of a big firm, a judge, or an aspiring law student looking for your advice and perspective.

The only goal I have for any networking event is to make a genuine connection with at least *one* person. This ensures that during each and every interaction, I am 100% focused on the person in front of me. When you are fully present, lead with questions that spark conversation (open-ended ones like "Can you tell me more about your practice?" are usually good icebreakers), engage in mindful listening,[22] and respond with enthusiasm, you are well on your way to forming a new, strong connection. Being fully present also keeps you from mindlessly scanning the room looking to find your next networking opportunity—a bad habit which no one on the receiving end ever appreciates.

The importance of making it easy to say "yes": *While writing this book, a current law student contacted me to help with my pre-publication review. The student was also interested in getting an internship at my current employer. In speaking with them, I realized an important fact. Some things are much easier for busy professionals to do or help with—to say "yes" to—than others. In general, it is much easier for me to say yes to a general career chat and share insights about my own work and career path than it is to help someone get a specific role at a specific company. This is important to keep in mind when you are reaching out to network with busy professionals. Is what you're asking for easy for them to say yes to? Be mindful of how you are framing the specific questions or requests for assistance in your communications. If you focus on just the question of "does your company have an internship opening," then the answer could be a quick and short "no"—or simply no response at all.*

LinkedIn has been an incredibly valuable tool for helping me build my professional network. The mission of LinkedIn is simple: "Connect the world's professionals to make them more productive and successful."[23] LinkedIn requires that you create a personal profile, which essentially functions as an interactive resume. It also allows you to send invitations to connect with other professionals on the platform, giving you the ability to directly message them. One of the most notable examples from my life of the benefits of LinkedIn is landing my current in-house dream job after a recruiter contacted me out of the blue to connect several years ago. And I wasn't even actively looking for new job opportunities at the time! There are a plethora of other platforms and options out there beyond LinkedIn, although none that I'm aware of that have the same critical mass of legal professionals.

While you are in law school, I also highly recommend taking time to join and participate in at least one student group in an area that genuinely interests you. Another great option is volunteering and/or engaging in pro bono activities. During law school I participated in a volunteer program called "Read To Me" to help underserved youth improve their literacy and phonics skills. I also took on a variety of different pro bono cases while practicing at law firms, including many focused on improving the lives of children. In terms of a more recent example, the very reason I'm writing this particular paragraph is due to feedback I received from an amazing immigration attorney that I recently met during a SEO Scholars[24] "speed networking" event.

How do you figure out where to start? I recommend being very **intentional** about who you want to connect with, and very **authentic** about why you are interested in connecting. This holds true regardless of whether you are connecting on LinkedIn, via email, or even in person. If the individual that you're reaching out to recently wrote a paper or article that intrigued you, then tell them. Is it a law professor that you admire? Let them know why. If the person tried an interesting case that you read about, it's worth mentioning that point when reaching out. It may sound simple, but your intention and how you communicate your interest makes all the difference, especially when trying to make a brand-new connection. While everyone is busy these days, most people are also interested in helping others—especially when they can get a real sense of your conviction and enthusiasm in having an opportunity to engage with them.

It doesn't take much: *As a practicing legal professional myself, I am much more likely to respond to even a short statement of interest or intent from a new connection than to a generic request. It can be something as simple as: "Your career path looks really relevant to some of my interests and I was motivated to contact you to see if we could connect so I could learn more about your background and experiences." Something generic, such as "I'm a 2L looking for a job," is going to generally result in fewer responses. In other words, take a bit of time to concisely articulate your curiosity about their background, where you are in your journey, and your interest in a short conversation to help inform potential next steps for your job search (or other goals). The key is to be genuine, sincere, and succinct. Make it obvious why you are asking to connect, and express gratitude for their time.*

Finally, a quick word about following up: it's important, even on LinkedIn (or whatever messaging platform you're using). As I previously noted, something short and sweet is always better than nothing. It could be as quick and friendly as: "Hi Dale: I really appreciate the time and connection earlier today. I will definitely look forward to future conversations!" To help get you started, the Additional Resources section at the end of this book includes examples of messages that I've sent in the past for reaching out to different types of potential connections on LinkedIn and through email.

THE BOTTOM LINE: Networking is really about paying attention to—and being more mindful of—your relationships and connections. It's impossible to predict how relationships that you form today will affect your life and legal journey tomorrow, but you should assume that many of these relationships can be impactful. From a purely professional standpoint, today's law school classmates are tomorrow's general counsels, hiring partners, judges, and elected officials. But the importance of personal connection can't be overstated—you might even be like me and find your life partner sitting next to you at law school orientation!

Regardless of your goals, remember that the most successful connections begin with genuine interest and curiosity versus a more "transactional" approach (think quality over quantity). While you don't need to go to every social or networking event, you shouldn't miss the opportunity while you are still *in* law school to start building your professional network for *after* law school. This includes connecting with your fellow classmates, as well as practicing legal professionals. These are connections that can last a lifetime, and that can open important doors for you in unexpected ways years from now. Don't wait—start using the other tools from the surthrival toolbox to prioritize and make a habit of regularly making new, genuine connections.

Surthrival Strategy #6:

FIND A PHILOSOPHY

RECOMMENDED TOOL: **STOICISM**

Find a set of guiding principles to help set your moral compass and weather any storm. As psychologist Abraham Maslow put it: "The human being needs a framework of values, a philosophy of life, a religion or religion-surrogate to live by and understand by, in about the same sense that he needs sunlight, calcium or love."[25]

Things don't always work out your way. Whether it's a bad grade, a bad illness, or just a bad day, it's critical to develop resiliency. Otherwise, these unfortunate things that inevitably happen in life can really throw you off your game.

When you do hit these rough patches, it is important to have some sort of higher-level principles to help you navigate the storm. This could be philosophy, religion, or really anything that helps you weather the adversity, stay strong, and keep putting one foot in front of the other. This type of personal growth and development—even in the hardest of circumstances—is how you can truly go from surviving to thriving in law school and in life.

In searching for how to be a better leader and how to live a more virtuous life, I recently stumbled across an ancient philosophy called Stoicism. To be honest, the extent of my knowledge about Stoic philosophy was literally the word itself, "stoic," and the fairly negative connotation that I associated with it. Yet the more I learned about Stoicism, the more I realized it could help me in ways that none of the other tools in this toolbox necessarily could. For me, the most important part of Stoicism is its focus on **what you can control**. This is known as the "dichotomy of control" in the pursuit of "eudaimonia," which translates[26] to happiness or human flourishing.

What makes this somewhat simple concept so powerful? Until I started studying Stoicism, I did not fully grasp how much time I spent worrying about things that *other people* were saying, doing, thinking, not thinking, or maybe could possibly think at some point. It's impossible to know these things, and the basic premise of Stoicism is that you should focus your energy on *your* actions, not what other people are doing.

As a practical matter with regards to law school, it means the important thing isn't how much time other people are spending on outlines but what *you yourself* are doing to prepare for your exams. At work, it means focusing on being as prepared as possible for your meetings, not worrying what others are doing as their preparation. And in relationships, it means focusing on how *you* are treating other people—not your perceptions of how they are treating you. If it's not something you can control, then you just don't spend time worrying about it. In fact, Stoics literally put everything outside their control into a bucket called "the indifferents."

I particularly like how Stoicism ties into mindfulness by focusing on the present moment. Since you can't control the past or the future, you can only control what you do right now. In every situation, you can't control what someone else does. But you can control your choices and your reaction to the person and situation. The focus of developing a healthy and virtuous life—and avoiding negativity because it's a waste of energy—has really helped change my mindset.

What's the best place to start if you're at the beginning of your Stoicism journey and/or just interested in learning a bit more? For me, the most helpful starting point was the aptly named book *The Beginner's Guide To Stoicism: Tools for Emotional Resilience & Positivity* by Matthew Van Natta. Here are a few examples of exercises from this great resource that have helped give me practical insight about what things I can actually control. See if these exercises can help give *you* perspective on any current challenges in your life.

- **Pause and compare:** If you're about to do something you really want to do (such as starting another episode of that show you're really into), try to find a way to delay making your decision (e.g., set a timer on your phone for one minute before starting the next episode). Then compare (i) doing what you wanted (the "pleasure") and how you'll feel making that choice versus (ii) making a more virtuous choice (a.k.a., "choosing excellence"), like spending that same twenty minutes studying or maybe even meditating.[27]

- **Circle yourself:** This is essentially a thought experiment in which you close your eyes and picture drawing a figurative circle around yourself to focus on what's within your control. In other words, try to separate out the things that you *can* control like your thoughts, actions, and desires (i.e., the things on the inside of this figurative "circle") from everything else going on in the world around you (i.e., "outside" the mental circle that you've "drawn" around yourself). For example, if you're starting to get stressed about an upcoming exam, take a deep breath and focus on what concrete steps you can take right now, such as reviewing your outline or taking a practice exam. By setting aside all of the outside influences you *aren't* able to control, it frees up headspace to focus and reflect on what's the best course of action that you can take right now.[28]

- **The view from above:** The point of this exercise is to give you perspective on life. As Van Natta explains in *The Beginner's Guide to Stoicism*: "Close your eyes and picture yourself from above. As you look at yourself, pull back and see your neighborhood. Then your town, your country, the world, perhaps even the universe. At each stage, put your challenges in relationship to what you are seeing. Notice that others are also confronting challenges. Allow your troubles to fade into the distance with this perspective. Find peace in the world."[29]

While I am far from considering myself a practicing Stoic, I can say with confidence that Stoic principles and practices have helped provide me with new tools for staying more centered as I navigate the many ups and downs of life. If you are ready to get help putting Stoic concepts into practice, Massimo Pigliucci's *A Handbook for New Stoics* has been another great practical resource.

THE BOTTOM LINE: The deeper you go in the surthrival toolbox, the more opportunity you have for deeper work on your personal growth and development. One way to go beyond surviving and get to thriving is by developing a consistent set of principles that serve as a personal compass to help you navigate challenging times. For some, this may be values from religion that you already practice; as just one example, core Quaker "SPICES" principles are Simplicity, Peace, Integrity, Community, Equality, and Stewardship. For others, it could be a bespoke set of guiding values that you memorialize in some form or fashion, like Ray Dalio has done in his book *Principles*. I've personally found that the ancient philosophy of Stoicism can provide these sorts of fundamental guiding principles. The focus of Stoicism on what you can control connects to mindfulness by helping you to focus on paying attention to the present versus worrying about what happened in the past or what's to come in the future. While Stoic philosophy has been helpful for me, the goal of this surthrival strategy is to do the work to find what philosophy will work best for you and truly help you bridge the transition from surviving to thriving.

Bonus Surthrival Strategy:

CONTINUE FINDING TOOLS

RECOMMENDED TOOLS: **CHOOSE YOUR OWN!**

Along your journey, unexpected challenges will undoubtedly arise. Many of the tools and strategies outlined in this guide will help prepare you for navigating these situations. But there is always more learning, growth, and development to do. Be sure to continue searching for the specific tools that will help you survive and thrive—both in law and in life.

The intention of this surthrival guide is to help you find tools and strategies that you can use to immediately improve your life. Being on this journey means you are guaranteed to face new challenges along the way. The tools in this surthrival toolbox are just a starting point. It's up to you to use the ones you need, set aside the ones that you don't, and continue actively searching for new tools that will help guide you on your personal path to surthriving.

Here's one recent example of my own. While writing this guide, I received startling news that I urgently needed to lose quite a bit of weight. A critical part of my path to successfully addressing this issue was quickly finding (and using) the right tools. This included discovering books (like Dr. Michael Greger's *How Not to Die* and *The How Not to Diet Cookbook*), as well as several free health and fitness apps (like MyFitnessPal, 7-Minute Workout, and Dr. Greger's Daily Dozen). From this eye-opening personal experience, I've learned that the tools you need are out there. You just have to keep searching for them and then be fully committed to embracing them.

Other examples? *When I was in law school, I had a hard time figuring out how to actually write a law exam—which is kind of a big problem. So, I found a tool called LEEWS*[30] *(Wentworth Miller's* ***L****aw* ***E****ssay* ***E****xam* ***W****riting* ***S****ystem). LEEWS taught me a basic methodology for how to structure and succeed on law school exams in a way that wasn't ever taught in my legal writing course. For you, a critical strategy might be finding the right bar exam prep course that will set you up for success after graduating, or perhaps finding the right LSAT prep tool before you even apply to law school.*

For any parents out there, I've found the Positive Discipline *series is an incredibly effective tool for helping to bring mindfulness to parenting. Or maybe you just want to work on being happier—who doesn't, right? Then read (or listen to)* Happier *by Harvard professor Tal Ben-Shahar, PhD.*

THE BOTTOM LINE: It is important to keep in mind that there are *many* other valuable tools and resources just waiting to be discovered. Because life is a journey, the tools that you'll need to surthrive won't remain fixed over time, and your work towards continuous self-improvement is never done. Getting advice from others about what has worked for them is often the best starting point. Whether health, happiness, holistic healing, or something else, being curious and open to trying new things is essential. The key is to continue searching for tools you can integrate into your life to make a difference and move the needle for *you*. After all this is your trip, and only you can decide where your journey will take you.

SURTHRIVAL CHECKLIST

Please visit the Surthriving Law website to download a free copy of this checklist.

To help you dive right into the tools and strategies, I have created this quick guide to the surthrival toolbox recommendations. If you do everything outlined below, you'll be well on your way to having an affordable, amazing set of tools to help you survive and thrive in law school (and beyond).

MINDFULNESS & MEDITATION

- ☐ Download the Headspace app, the Calm app, or another meditation app of your choosing.
- ☐ Meditate for at least two minutes a day this week.

BUDGETING

- ☐ Download the You Need A Budget app or budgeting app of your choosing.
- ☐ Create your first budget and link at least one bank account.

HABITIZING

- ☐ Read or listen to *Atomic Habits* by James Clear.
- ☐ Write down one new positive habit you will do for at least two minutes a day for the next thirty days—meditating counts! Try "stacking" it right after a current habit or making it part of something that's already in your daily routine, like brushing your teeth.

ORGANIZING & PRIORITIZING

- ☐ Order the Productivity Planner, the Self Journal, or use the free template found in Chapter 4.
- ☐ Write down one (and only one) #1 priority per day.

NETWORKING

- ☐ Sign up for a free account on LinkedIn. Already have an account? Make sure it is up to date, accurate, and best represents your professional journey!
- ☐ Send a connection request with a "personalized invite" to at least one person every Friday this month.

PHILOSOPHIZING

- ☐ Read *The Beginner's Guide to Stoicism* by Matthew Van Natta or *A Handbook for New Stoics* by Massimo Pigliucci.
- ☐ Start working through the short exercises (or similar ones from a different philosophy).

FIND YOUR OWN!

- ☐ After working through these tasks, it may be time to start searching for additional tools specific to your personal needs and/or interests.
- ☐ Need an idea? I recommend downloading Dr. Greger's Daily Dozen app from Apple's App Store or Google Play Store to work on improving personal nutrition habits.

A FINAL THOUGHT ON THE SURTHRIVAL TOOLBOX AND NOTE ON THE REMAINING SECTIONS

My goal with Part I was to provide you with a strong foundation for facing life's challenges, whether it's your first legal exam, your first bar exam, your first day at a law firm, or your first court appearance—you get the idea. As we figuratively close the lid on the surthrival toolbox (at least for now), I hope that my focus on tools I have found impactful in my life will help make starting the journey to surthriving law school—and life—as easy as possible for you on yours.

***Career Context:** Throughout the rest of this book, I will provide context of my own path to give you a better sense about what experiences have helped form—and inform—my perspectives and advice. I will start with some of the places where my career journey took me before law school. Later in this guide, guest contributors will also share context on their own backgrounds.*

MY PRE-LAW JOURNEY (IN A NUTSHELL):

- Grew up in Northern California and went to public schools (Davis, CA).
- Worked as a manager at McDonald's in high school (Davis, CA).
- Attended college in Southern California at UCLA (Los Angeles, CA).
- Worked miscellaneous jobs in college (library, law firms, compliance training start-up).
- Participated in the California State Assembly Fellowship Program after graduating from UCLA (Sacramento, CA).
- Worked as a field organizer on a U.S. presidential campaign (Iowa and Michigan).
- Started a (fun but unprofitable and now dissolved) poker clothing company.
- Took a summer trip to Europe before law school with money saved from a side job.
- Attended law school orientation at Northwestern University School of Law (Chicago, IL).

Part II

YOUR LEGAL JOURNEY BEGINS

Every legal journey starts with a decision about whether to take the LSAT and apply to law school. If you have not made that decision yet—or know someone who is currently wrestling with it—you can find my personal perspective on that incredibly important decision in the appendix. For everyone who is already in law school (or committed to going), the following section features additional strategies and perspectives to help change your mindset from just getting through it to truly making the most of it—and maybe even having some fun along the way!

Chapter 8

SURTHRIVING IN LAW SCHOOL

If you dive right into law school without the tools you need for prioritizing and staying organized, things can get overwhelming pretty quickly. This section outlines additional strategies for surthriving in law school beyond the surthrival toolbox from Part I. It also includes the perspectives of several current law school students who have contributed their insight and advice on everything from navigating law school during a pandemic, to staying ahead of your 1L readings, to exploring public interest law.

***Totally overwhelmed.* That's how** I felt in my first year of law school. And my second year. Even when most of my classmates seemed to be taking it easy during their third year, I was busy (and exhausted) re-interviewing for law firm jobs, publishing my note on the implications of multi-jurisdictional merger review,[31] and serving as an Executive Editor for Northwestern Law's *Journal of International Law and Business*. I was also struggling with the emotional stress of having my younger half-sister, Hannah, diagnosed with brain cancer just as my third year of law school was starting. If you are feeling overwhelmed or dealing with any similar challenges, know that you are not alone. In fact, being overwhelmed is one of the things that I consistently continue to hear that current law students are struggling to deal with. What's worse is that for the most part, it can feel like you're on your own to figure out what to do about it and how to make it better. The good news is that it actually doesn't have to be that way. Let's talk about some of the concrete steps that you can start taking right now to help you overcome these difficulties.

A key part of finding more balance and better navigating the many competing priorities of law school is using the tools from the surthrival toolbox in Part I. I really can't emphasize this enough. While doing research for this book, I learned through surveys that many current students were familiar with meditation and some already use the recommended apps. While mindfulness is a critical first step, it's also just the first step. Virtually none of the students that I surveyed had heard of or used the tools that I've recommended for creating better habits, budgeting, and focusing on top priorities. I've come to learn that these are all *absolutely essential* ingredients for staying afloat in terms of both mental and physical health during stressful times, which includes not just law school but much of the practice of law after you graduate.

The best part is that *it doesn't take much time or money* to start implementing these changes. I know how busy life gets in law school (and the current students reminded me of this, as well). But here's the thing. You are going to be so much more focused and efficient with your time after using these tools that the time and energy you invest in using them will start paying dividends within weeks, if not days. You are also setting yourself up with a healthier and more sustainable approach to work–life balance before you even start your professional career, where you'll face even more demands, pressures, and stresses. So if you skipped Part I, then please go back and read it, or at least skim the Surthrival Checklist found on pages 62 to 64, and which is also available on the Surthriving Law website.

But enough about the toolbox for now. Let's look at several additional tips, tools, and strategies I highly recommend adopting during law school.

FIND A MENTOR

Law school does not have to be a solo expedition, but it often felt like one to me. I found myself frequently looking around and mimicking what others were doing because I wasn't sure what I was actually "supposed" to be doing, or how to do it. For some reason it failed to occur to me that everyone else was doing essentially the same thing. I really wish that someone had told me about the importance of seeking outside perspectives and guidance while you are in law school. During that time, I would have greatly benefited from consulting with a practicing lawyer already doing the type of work that I was most interested in doing myself. In other words, I needed a mentor and you probably do, too.

Mentors are experienced and trusted advisors. They are usually someone within the legal profession who has already "been there, done that" and can help you navigate difficult decisions. That's exactly why it's extremely important to find one (or more) of them as soon as you can.

Good mentors typically have the following qualities:[32]

- **The right mindset**—namely, a true interest in giving their time, effort, and energy to helping others succeed. This is by far the most important quality of a good mentor, because when someone is genuinely invested in you, the remaining elements in this list will come naturally.
- **An ability to dedicate time and space** in their schedules for connecting with you. It's not enough just to want to support you; they need to be able to actually

allocate consistent time for building a relationship. I personally recommend connecting monthly if possible, and once per quarter as an absolute minimum commitment during the course of a year.

- **Experience, connections, and knowledge** that are relevant to you and your interests.
- **A commitment to being real**, including sharing both successes and teachable moments from their own journey. They should also express interest in learning from you.
- **Prior experience** helping to develop and mentor others is an added plus.

How do you find a mentor? In my experience, it's unfortunately easier to determine you need a mentor than to actually find one. An important strategy is to try to make connections and develop relationships. Sometimes there are formal programs at your school or company that pair you with a mentor. For example, I still participate in a formal mentor program run by the UCLA Alumni Association every year. These types of arrangements can be hit or miss as they totally depend on the mentor–mentee relationship and connection. Good mentors can come from a variety of other places. Sometimes they are family friends. They might be a favorite law professor or even just an alumnus from your school that you found on LinkedIn. It might take some effort, and more than a few attempts, but it will be well worth the time invested.

PERIODICALLY REFLECT ON YOUR BIG PICTURE GOALS & PRIORITIES

There's something to be said about the phrase: "begin with the end in mind." If you already know what you are passionate about and plan to focus on after law school, then you are probably ahead of the curve. This allows you to choose what activities to prioritize based on how they align with your goals during law school. If you are not exactly sure what's in store for you after law school, that's probably how the person in front of you and behind you in class are feeling, too. It's *really* hard to know, particularly because most of law school oddly isn't focused on the actual practice of law. That's why finding a mentor is the first step. It's also part of the reason that I put together this guide and sought out guest contributors. There's just no substitute for finding and connecting with people who are doing something that you think you are interested in doing, which is why networking is an important part of the surthrival toolbox.

But let's get back to you. If you aren't proactive about reflecting on and trying to define your goals, you might just end up going along with what everyone else at your law school is doing. At Northwestern Law, that generally meant trying to get jobs at large law firms. Speaking from personal experience, this can lead to an unhappy career path; for example, you could end up getting stuck doing something that you're not actually very interested in doing in order to pay off student loan debt. One solution is to proactively pause and reflect on what you're interested in doing, what you're passionate about, and what matters the most to you in life. Try using the worksheet that I have provided at the end of this section to help with this exercise. You can also use one of the planners recommended in Part I for these periodic career reflections, whether before, during, or even after law school.

LEARN TO SAY "YES, AND" (VERSUS OVERLOADING OR OVERCOMMITTING)

For me, another unfortunate by-product of not mapping out a specific plan or career path was overcommitment. Trying to keep as many options open as possible led to trying to do *all* of the things possible. This in turn led to lots of stress and anxiety but very little sleep. This fear of commitment to a particular path resulted in a very scattered, overextended, and stressful life.

I know how hard it is to say no to potentially helpful career opportunities during law school, I really do. Instead, I would recommend trying out a trick from the world of improv comedy. The improv trick is saying "yes, and..." versus "no." This way, you don't ever automatically shut the door on anything, but it gives you the space to say: "**Yes**, I'd love to work on that, **and** I could definitely get to it after finals are over, if that's okay?" The more that you are developing positive habits and paying attention to how you are prioritizing your time, the more realistic you can be when using this "yes, and" trick.

PURSUIT OF PERFECTION— KNOW WHEN TO LET GO

Even after you prioritize and determine what to focus on, you still have to figure out how much time to spend actually doing it. During law school it was incredibly hard for me to know when something was "done." Whether it was outlining for class, writing a brief for my first-year legal writing course, or preparing for exams, I felt like I could keep revising, tweaking, and updating indefinitely. I've found this is equally true after you graduate, whether you're writing an actual brief for a court filing, preparing for a deposition, or trying to write a guide like this one. It's just the nature of the work, which is inherently subjective. If you have a streak of perfectionism like I do—and I suspect that I'm in good company here—then it can take a tremendous toll on you if you are willing to forgo sleep, exercise, and a host of other healthy habits to instead put more hours into a never-ending quest to get your final work product just right. Decide how much time you can realistically give to a particular task and then actually stick to whatever that time frame is.

The more that you can practice setting boundaries in law school, the better off you will be at setting boundaries in life after law school. That means holding yourself accountable when allocating time to work on something. If you're going to work until 10 p.m., then actually work until 10 p.m. and get some sleep (okay, maybe a few minutes after 10 p.m. is fine, but you get the point). For anyone with a significant other in your life, this is even more important as they're counting on you to keep your agreements in your relationship. Candidly, this is an area that I still struggle with (just ask my partner), but focusing on mindfulness and self-awareness (plus all the other tools from Part I) really do help. This is definitely (ultra) marathon, not sprint, territory and something that I'm trying to continuously work on improving while not being too hard on myself for any misses or course corrections needed along the way.

A reflection on letting it go: *Nothing is permanent. You'll always have more assignments, more exams, and more work to do. For example, I hoped to include additional guest contributions from a judge, a law professor, and a general counsel in this guide. But it was also important to balance how much time I had for the overall project (not* *much), when the next year of law school was starting (soon), and opportunities for future editions (plenty). I'll also keep working on including more voices from perspectives historically underrepresented in the legal profession. This is all part of the journey for me, and there is a lot to be said for actually completing something when it's good enough (which hopefully this is), and putting it out there. Try to do the best you can with the time you can dedicate to something, and then be okay with moving on when it's time to let it go and turn to the next thing. It will be okay. You got this.*

FIND YOUR OUTLETS AND HAVE (MORE) FUN

You can be more efficient and productive using the time you have allocated for work when you also allocate time for stress outlets and just having fun. Don't believe it? Just look at the studies[33] directly linking productivity to happiness. As soon as you're starting to feel burned out, that is the time to pause and disconnect to do something to help you recharge and come back refreshed. For some people that thing is exercise or meditation. For others it might be cooking or playing an instrument. Whatever it is for you, find it and do whatever you can to prioritize doing it.

I have definitely been guilty of taking things too seriously, and I still often do (as anyone who knows me will tell you). But if you're stressed and anxious during law school, remember that you will likely have no shortage of things to be stressed and anxious about after you graduate—so why not build in time for some fun? If there's something you have a passion for that's been pushed to the side or put on hold, you can pick it back up today. Don't wait! If you're anything like me, you might already be sacrificing more than you think.

DON'T BE AFRAID TO ASK FOR HELP

This last step might be the most difficult, but also the most important. You are not alone and people want to help support you. Just recently I saw someone poignantly post on LinkedIn: **"Ask for help. It's brave."**[34] They're right. It takes courage to ask. But when the waters get choppy—as they did for this individual—the smartest thing to do is find a life vest to stay afloat. There are a variety of places for you to turn: therapists and counselors, friends and family, mentors and other outside advisors. Just start somewhere, with someone.

THE BOTTOM LINE: The more clarity you have about where you're going *after* law school, the more focused you can be about how you spend your time *during* law school. This doesn't mean that you have to know exactly what you want to do after you graduate. But it does involve some time and effort on your part—namely, reflecting on what you're truly interested in doing, and making time to connect with mentors and other legal professionals who can offer you support, guidance, and perspective. Know that many (if not most) other law students feel the same way you do, and don't hesitate to ask for help when you need it. Remember, it's a marathon, not a sprint, and you need to pace yourself and have some fun along the way.

PERSONAL GOALS & PRIORITIES

Try using this worksheet to begin mapping out ideas for developing better clarity regarding your own goals and priorities. Remember that you can always come back to update your answers!

Step 1: Create a "Personal Priority List" using the below suggestions or other ideas that are important to you to fill out in the "Personal Priority List" table.

- Mental/physical health
- Having fun/joyful life
- Seeing friends
- Strong family relationships
- Getting good grades
- Being happy
- Creating meaningful connections
- Other: ____________________

Personal Priority List*

Top Priority ____

2nd Priority ____

3rd Priority ____

**The number of priorities is intentionally limited here to ensure you have time to actually prioritize them!*

Step 2: Write down your main goals for (i) during law school, and (ii) after law school.

My main goal DURING law school is: ______________________

____

____

____

My main goal AFTER law school is: ______________________

____

____

____

Step 3: When feeling overwhelmed, review your to-do list to see if what you're doing is consistent with everything that you've written down on this worksheet. If not, consider taking one (or more) of the following actions:

1. Find a mentor
2. Reflect on your big-picture goals & priorities
3. Try saying "yes, and"
4. Let it go—it doesn't have to be perfect
5. Remember your outlets for stress & fun
6. Don't be afraid to ask for help

Chapter 9

CURRENT LAW STUDENT PERSPECTIVES

It seemed absolutely essential to get feedback from current law students and incoming JD candidates before publishing this guide. After all, there would be no point pressing ahead with putting out a guide that wasn't actually useful. By adopting a mindset that feedback is a gift, I embraced the insights that these busy students were willing to share with me (and yes, the irony of asking law students to add something else to their very full plates was definitely acknowledged and mitigated to the extent that I could). I came to realize that the best way to address some of the challenges they were facing was by sharing their perspectives directly.

CURRENT 1L PERSPECTIVE

GUEST CONTRIBUTOR: **ANONYMOUS 1L (HARVARD LAW SCHOOL)**

Author's note: This student's story spoke to me because of their calm and poised approach that I wish I had taken myself during my 1L year. When speaking with this individual, I was particularly impressed with how there was a palpable absence of stress. Their story and perspective underscores to me the importance of (i) finding the particular tools that work for you; (ii) sticking with consistent habits and rituals to keep you on track and not get overloaded; and (iii) how the choices you make about what's important to you and how to spend your time have a huge impact on your overall well-being.

I am a current 1L at Harvard Law School. Law school was a predictable destination for me simply because of my nature and strengths, and while the path was winding and somewhat protracted, it led where it was supposed to. I'm the type that had fun with the LSATs and I really appreciate good statutory analysis or a classic Scalia exposition on the importance of the separation of powers. But don't worry, most people in my class are totally normal!

The biggest piece of advice I would give to a 0L [an incoming JD candidate] is to stay ahead of your obligations. I started reading for classes about a week before each semester started and made it my goal to maintain that cushion as best I could throughout the semester. Instead of reading each night for the next day's class, I was reading for class the next week. By reading ahead I never had to fret about being totally unprepared for a class and I knew that if I really needed to, I could take a day—or even two—off during the semester at no cost. Best of all, at the end of the semester, when the rest of my classmates were reading for the final week of class, I was getting a head start on preparation for the all-important finals.

Staying a week ahead of readings does make you a little less fresh for cold calls [*Author's note: This is a reference to the somewhat dreaded "Socratic method" employed by professors in many first-year law school classes*] but by doing a quick review before class I found that I was usually well equipped to answer most questions. Anyway, as you quickly find out in law school, cold calls mean absolutely nothing in the grand scheme of things [*Author's note: This is due to the fact that your entire grade is often based solely on exam performance versus other factors*]. I happily traded better cold calls for a stress-free semester.

To keep myself on schedule I bought a jumbo wall calendar and would pencil in the readings I had planned for the upcoming week each Sunday night. Right below that calendar on the wall was my weekly planner (built using a free internet template) which I created as soon as I got a sense of how long the readings took me. I designed a weekly schedule that accounted for class and carved out times to do each of my readings throughout the week. Each day I knew which time slots were carved out for readings. As I finished each reading (and typed up my notes) I would circle off that reading on my calendar.

THE BOTTOM LINE: By sticking to my schedule and having a clear idea of when I was going to do everything, I managed a stress-free 1L! I hope that sharing these tips will help you as well.

CURRENT 2L PERSPECTIVE

GUEST CONTRIBUTOR: **MAGDALENE BEDI**

(UC HASTINGS COLLEGE OF THE LAW)

Author's note: Magdalene's experience deeply resonated with me because it acknowledged the unspoken but very real sense that you have to do it all. It can be so hard to figure out on your own where it makes the most sense to focus your time and effort, which is why outside advisors and mentors can be so incredibly helpful for law students. I also admire the courageous decision to actually scale back and take a "yes, and" approach. It's easier said than done but the sooner you can begin to flex that muscle the better because these types of pressures can be the same or even greater after you graduate and have started your career as a practicing lawyer.

I first heard about this project through a classmate and decided to share feedback with Adam via a survey link that he had circulated. I was interested in learning more because there's an excess of advice for law students, of varying quality. But when advice is good, its impact is huge; good advice has made me a better student, a better peer, and a better advocate. I was curious to see Adam's approach, but

I was also eager to offer my own perspectives on advice that has worked, advice that hasn't worked, and advice I'm still craving.

For context, I am currently a 2L at UC Hastings College of the Law, and I attended American University where I studied Communications, Legal Institutions, Economics, and Government. I first became interested in law when I sued my public high school for hosting mandatory religious assemblies. My experiences as a teenage plaintiff created a lasting impression that I explored through pre-law courses, and then as a paralegal at a workers' compensation law firm after graduation.

I knew law school would be difficult; I was aware of troubling statistics and I'd sought mentorship from practicing attorneys who'd offered their own anecdotes. Placing hundreds of high-achieving, hardworking students in a competitive atmosphere inevitably breeds insecurity and stress. Still, I couldn't have anticipated the intensity of that stress until my first year. Stress that, I believe, is largely caused by poor boundaries, overcommitment, and an inability to say "no."

For example, I joined moot court to improve my legal writing skills, and because I enjoy oral advocacy. I competed in the fall of my 2L year and joined the board in spring. Our board members are required to either compete on a team or coach a team for one of the intercollegiate competitions we attend. Additionally, we are required to assist a Legal Writing and Research course, attend weekly board meetings, judge at least twenty oral argument practices for other competing teams, and take on a "board task," which is usually some sort of 1L outreach initiative. Competing entails co-writing an appellate brief and attending at least twenty-five oral argument practices, which are scheduled and moderated by coaches.

It is a substantial commitment. But students often feel pressured to also extern or join a journal or pursue leadership in other organizations in addition to moot court. Everyone's limits vary. But students who have attempted to extern or engage in other extracurriculars while competing on a team have described it to me as a miserable experience. Those same students will quickly add, "but it's possible."

What's "possible" is not always what's "productive." I've witnessed team members break down into tears during oral argument practices because constructive feedback was the straw that broke their backs after weeks of balancing a bloated schedule on minimal sleep. I've experienced the frustration of compensating for a colleague that couldn't complete their portion of a group deliverable because they were too overwhelmed with other obligations. And I've also forced colleagues to compensate for my own absences when I've bitten off more than I can chew. In both circumstances, our final product suffered.

There is nothing gained from an experience where you can't perform because you're spread too thin. It damages your relationships, and it harms your reputation as a professional. It prevents you from being flexible when unexpected emergencies arise or when a more compelling opportunity comes up. More importantly, it feels awful.

I valued my time in moot court, but as I approach my final year in law school there are other opportunities I want to pursue. I chose to embrace Adam's "yes, and" approach by leaving moot court but staying involved with UC Hastings' Legal Writing and Research department in a limited capacity. After I communicated my intention to leave, I had a few conversations with other students who also either wanted to leave or wanted to limit their engagement somehow but found they couldn't say "no" or "yes, and." This experience, above any other so far, highlighted for me how difficult it is for law students to acknowledge their limits.

While I'm also still working on setting boundaries and balancing my own schedule, there are two approaches I've found helpful in mitigating the discomfort of acknowledging my limits in law school.

First, I schedule in fun by setting time aside for my hobbies outside of law school. When I'm planning out my semester, I have the urge to fill every blank space on my calendar. But when I mark space off as dedicated to something I enjoy, it's no longer "free" for me to schedule over. Thus, I limit my commitments while also ensuring I have something to look forward to even during periods where I'm overwhelmed by stress that can't be avoided, such as during midterm season.

And if I need to be flexible later in the semester, I have some wiggle room to rearrange my schedule or add to my schedule because of the space I set aside.

Second, I seek out my mentors when I need objectivity. Often, law students overload their schedules because they fear the consequences of rejecting opportunities, or because they worry about falling behind. When I find myself unsure if I'm on the right track, I reach out to one of my mentors and ask their opinion. Talking with someone who has undergone and survived the ordeal of law school quiets the noise that can build when you're surrounded by students who are just as anxious and just as busy as you. If you're unsure where to find mentorship, there is no better place to start than in your professor's office hours.

THE BOTTOM LINE: Some stress can't be avoided. But if you judiciously manage your time and acknowledge your limitations, law school is an exciting opportunity to dive headfirst into your personal and professional development. I've adored exploring interests I'd never had the resources or mentorship to consider before. Law school introduced me to a passion for copyright and trademark law, and because of law school I have classmates and professors who are more than happy to geek out over both with me. Law school is challenging, but it can and should be fun, too.

CURRENT 3L PERSPECTIVE: BIGLAW TRACK

GUEST CONTRIBUTOR: **ANONYMOUS 3L**

(TOP 14 LAW SCHOOL, AS RANKED BY *U.S. NEWS & WORLD REPORT* MAGAZINE)

Author's note: This student had a 100% virtual summer associate program, and was willing to share what that experience was like. Interestingly, the importance of proactively seeking out individuals at the firm was just as relevant in the virtual environment for this student as I found it to be in the pre-pandemic (100% in-person) summer program.

I'm currently a 3L student and the COVID-19 pandemic began midway through my 2L spring, [while I was] in school. When reading an early draft of this book, it struck me that there wasn't a whole lot of advice or insight about what it's like actually being in law school and working as a summer associate in the middle of a pandemic.

Before turning to the summer program, I just want to touch briefly on my general experience of being a law student during the pandemic as compared to 1L year. Putting aside the stress of quickly moving during the middle of the semester, there have been both benefits and drawbacks to attending "virtual" law school. One opportunity that I found was the ability to do work remotely that would have otherwise been unavailable [to me]. For instance, I was able to do a remote internship at a state attorney general's office located far away from the location of my actual law school. Similarly, I was able to make a bit of extra money by doing more research assistant work for professors in the extra hours each day ([hours available] from not doing the normal in-person law school activities). Having pointed out some of the benefits, I think it is also important to note the drawbacks. I've found it's harder to get to know other students and professors in the virtual environment. Beyond that, I think there are some additional stressors around exams and grades during COVID-19. It can feel a bit lonely to study and prepare on your own, instead of on campus with other students all doing the same thing. I found an effective technique to help manage this stress was reaching out to others in class to do practice exams and study together over video call.

I have also seen and spoken with other classmates who are feeling even more stressed and anxious as the pandemic has dragged on. Many of my classmates are interested in working at large law firms, and law firm hiring has felt remarkably uncertain over the past twelve months. This naturally can create more concern for students, especially with the news of canceled summer programs or delayed associate start dates post-graduation. Speaking of jobs, I went through a "normal" on-campus interviewing process pre-pandemic. For that reason, I can't speak directly to what virtual OCI is like. But I did just finish a 100% virtual summer associate program for a large law firm in New York City.

Most of the benefits and drawbacks of 100% remote law school apply to an internship, as well. It was tough to get to know the other summers [summer interns] in my cohort (even with Zoom trivia and that sort of thing) and likewise with the other associates at the firm. Something about a virtual coffee just doesn't result in as candid of a conversation as the same interaction in person. That being said, it was also much easier to seek out and work for specific people within the firm, even if they were in a different office. I specifically requested to work with a partner who had a background in government service, as I knew he would be a good mentor should I decide to take that path in the future. Getting the chance to work for that specific partner was one of the things that attracted me to the firm in the first place, and I think it definitely was worthwhile even with things being virtual.

Another one of the biggest impacts from having a virtual summer program was it just being a lot of work. I bring this up not to complain at all, as the compensation is phenomenal, particularly while so many others have been impacted by the pandemic. But the point here is that students should expect *much* less emphasis on social activities than what I've heard about how summer programs used to be. Maybe as a result of this, my law firm shortened the summer internship, perhaps realizing that a virtual program resulted in much more true "work" and much less socializing or learning about the firm.

Here are some other specific things about the whole process that I wish I had known as a 1L:

- It can be difficult to get a feel for the different practice areas during a virtual internship, so try to do as much of the work of deciding what kind of lawyer you'd like to be ahead of time—be it through conversations, reading about the different types of work, or your 1L summer job.

- Leverage your school's network before going into the interview process. Talking to alumni will often result in more candid conversations, and it will let you think through your options without the time pressure of the interview process.

- Don't be disappointed if you don't end up at *the* law firm you had as your top choice—odds are you'll find people you really enjoy working with at most law firms, and if that's not the case, plenty of people re-recruit as 3Ls, as well.

In terms of final thoughts reflecting on this entire experience, I think the most important thing I want to convey is even though it can be difficult to build new relationships in virtual school or law firm work, it's still important to reach out for help or mentorship during stressful times. Whether this is someone you knew from before or someone you've only seen on the screen, I think you'll find they're more receptive to help out than you'd imagine!

THE BOTTOM LINE: Virtual law school opens up new opportunities, but also is uniquely stressful. Do your best to make the most of it by doing things you couldn't otherwise do, and reaching out to friends and classmates for support during these stressful times. Similarly, a virtual internship can feel like it's missing a lot of the glitz and glamour you might expect, but that doesn't mean you can't try to build relationships and learn about the firm via video call. Don't be afraid to reach out—you'll probably find that the person on the other side of the email is happy to talk with you!

CURRENT 3L PERSPECTIVE: NON-BIGLAW TRACK

GUEST CONTRIBUTOR: **NATALIE HOLLABAUGH**
(LEWIS & CLARK LAW SCHOOL)

Author's note: I was reminded by a number of current students that there are many different paths that bring people to law school, and that there are paths that people take after graduating which do not involve law firms of any shape or size. I made a genuine effort to expand the perspectives shared beyond my own and make this guide as broadly relevant and inclusive as I could. I'm very grateful that Natalie was willing to share her public interest journey. For further perspectives on career tracks outside of BigLaw, please be sure to see Part VI ("Beyond BigLaw"), which includes a guest contribution from a practicing public interest attorney.

My name is Natalie Hollabaugh and I am a third-year student at Lewis & Clark Law School in Portland, Oregon. I was a public school teacher before law school, and plan to pursue a career in public interest law, specifically juvenile justice, after graduating. I agreed to share my perspective after reviewing a pre-publication draft of the manuscript and noting the relative lack of focus on careers outside of the author's own experience. To my surprise, Adam asked me to share a bit about my own journey and insight for others out there who might be interested in exploring legal careers focused on public interest law.

Part of what brought me to Lewis & Clark is the ability to pursue a path in public interest in an environment that was very collegial. Many of my classmates were also interested in the same things I was. I currently serve as a Staff Member for the Youth Legal Clinic which is part of the Criminal Justice Reform Clinic. In this role I work directly with youth who are incarcerated and make sure they know their rights after they have been convicted or adjudicated. I am also President of the Public Interest Law Project (PILP) on campus. My work in PILP helps me remain connected to the public interest community both on campus and in the greater Portland area, and allows me to raise funds for students like myself to pursue this work.

So how will you know if a public interest career path makes sense for you? For me, it was a few things.

It's important to emphasize that it doesn't have to be all or nothing. One small step to take is to begin by volunteering with a nonprofit that's doing important work in an area that you find meaningful. Whether that is environmental, education, voting rights, or racial injustice issues, these organizations are *always* looking for additional support and typically welcome volunteer contributions. Your school may even have resources to connect you with people, but also do not be afraid to reach out "cold" and express your interest in helping out.

In terms of practical advice, another part of the equation that often comes up is money. If you have huge student loans it can make pursuing this type of career a bit scary, to be honest, especially so if you do not have a financial safety net (which is most of us). It's safe to say that most people who follow a path to public interest law aren't doing it for the money. But when I think about the impact that I can have doing something I love, it more than makes up for the financial element. I have carefully planned out how to balance scholarships and student loans, and have plotted out my path to Public Interest Student Loan Forgiveness in the future. Try to be proactive in looking for summer funding, too, and know if you're in a pinch you can always try to get school credit for your public interest positions while in law school.

I also want to shed some light on how to figure out what types of organizations actually hire public interest lawyers, and what my approach to finding a job after law school has been. I think that the best place to start is a little harder to pinpoint than BigLaw. For most, the public interest hiring "cycle" is very unclear or does not exist. Outside of fellowships, which have very strict timelines, public interest jobs can be posted in the fall of your final year all the way through to the summer after graduation. I think the best advice is to be ready early and be prepared for a longer job hunt than others. For fellowships, if you think you might be interested in some of the larger public interest fellowships (like Skadden or Equal Justice Works), start researching these your second year of school so you don't miss any important deadlines and can start the long applications with plenty of time.

Here are some specific things about the whole experience of working in this field that I wish I had known before applying to law school:

- Research funding options for summer positions and future internships in advance so you can plan ahead for when and how to apply for supplemental funds.
- Have a backup plan in case you cannot get supplemental funds.
- It is very easy to get discouraged from doing this work because of the financial piece. Before you walk away, reach out to folks on your campus and in the community. Some of the best financial and planning advice I got was from current career public interest attorneys. And you can always reach out to connect with me directly via LinkedIn.
- Public interest jobs can be demanding and emotional. Making sure you have a steady well of energy and

empathy to draw from will be key, so keeping that well full and replenished is really important. Personally, getting outside and cooking are both ways I relieve stress and practice self-care.

Finally, Adam asked me to touch on any other advice about how I manage to balance a number of different commitments during law school without overcommitting and stretching myself too thin. During the course of the past (almost) three years of law school, I have learned that there is always time for doing the things that matter most to you. You just have to be extremely diligent about knowing *what* your own priorities actually are and *how* you are actually spending your time every day. That's why I think the surthrival toolbox discussed in Part I of this guide can be incredibly useful. Beyond those areas already covered, based on my own experience I would suggest scheduling out most of your time, including time relaxing, time with friends or family, appointments, etcetera. By laying everything out, including little things I maybe was not accounting for, it allowed me to see what, if any, free time I had so I could make sure I wasn't overcommitting when I said yes to something.

In terms of final thoughts reflecting on this entire experience, I think the most important thing for you to know about exploring a career in public interest is that it is absolutely worth it. I might not be graduating with the promise of a six-figure paycheck but I am graduating with my dream job. This will allow me to continue to center directly impacted people in my daily work; for me, all the work of law school led up to this moment.

THE BOTTOM LINE: Pursuing public interest law during law school (and beyond) is incredibly worthwhile, so don't let the financial piece deter you from something that you are truly passionate about. It takes a little creativity and a lot of hard work, but you can find your dream job doing work that you will love for communities and individuals who deserve excellent representation. I can't recommend this path highly enough!

Part III

LET'S GET A JOB!

While in law school, I'm not sure anything takes up more collective time—or generates more anxiety—in law students than finding a job. I know that much of my time and effort during law school was spent trying to decipher what felt like a sometimes impossible code to crack: What does it take to get hired by large law firms, or any legal employer, for that matter?

You can benefit from my process of trial and error (emphasis on the "error" part). Over the course of over a hundred interviews where I was on both sides of the interview table, I have developed a strong sense of the key ingredients for successful interviewing.

While the following strategies and tips are based mostly on my own interviews and observations with large law firms, I am confident that this approach will help you be well prepared for virtually any type of interview. At the end of the day, at a basic level most interviewers are all trying to figure out the same questions: "Do I want to take a chance on hiring this person? Do they have what it takes to succeed here?" As you'll see, you actually have more control in shaping the answers to those questions than you might think. So let's get right to it!

Author's note: As indicated in the Preface, at the time of publication (June 2021), ongoing COVID-related concerns continue to upend many areas of our lives. While the mechanics of interviewing currently look different (e.g., lots of video calls), I have included my approach to the "traditional" model for now as I think much of the advice is still quite useful and relevant. To the extent there are lasting changes to the overall firm recruiting process, I will be sure to provide advice and guidance on the Surthriving Law website, as well as in future editions of this guide.

Career Context: *Here is a look at the next stage of my legal journey during law school and in the world of large law firms. My advice on interviewing in the following section is based on my experience interviewing—and getting hired—for these positions.*

MY LAW SCHOOL JOB SEARCH (IN A NUTSHELL):

- 1L Summer: Government/public service (DOJ Antitrust, Washington, D.C.) with Student Funded Public Interest Fellowships (SFPIF) grant from Northwestern Law.
- 2L OCI: Participated in on-campus interviewing.
- 2L Summer: BigLaw—Summer associate in NYC office of Heller Ehrman, a CA-based firm. The firm went from being on the *American Lawyer* magazine's "A List" of Top 20 law firms to declaring bankruptcy during my third (3L) year of law school.
- 3L OCI: Participated in on-campus interviewing again as a 3L. Ultimately accepted an offer to join NYC-based Sullivan & Cromwell as a first-year associate.
- 3L Semester: Externed for the Hon. Sidney Schenkier (Magistrate) as part of a judicial practicum.

Chapter 10

A SIMPLE SOLUTION FOR SUCCESS

The single most impactful thing you can do to ace any interview—regardless of the employer—is figuring out how to tell a compelling story about your career journey and why working for this specific firm/company/organization is an exceptionally interesting and genuinely exciting opportunity for you. This requires more preparation and "due diligence" than you might expect, especially in two key areas: (i) making sure that you have done enough research about the potential employer and people who will be interviewing you; and (ii) creating a short but thoughtful set of three to four key talking points to keep you focused on your message, allowing you to emphasize the things most likely to help you get an offer.

Recruiting for the nation's largest law firms (BigLaw) is still done through a somewhat archaic process at law schools known as on-campus interviewing or "OCI" (but also known by a variety of other acronyms depending on which law school you attend). Candidates fortunate enough to survive the gauntlet of dreaded twenty-minute OCI interviews are rewarded with a coveted "callback"—a series of slightly longer (approximately thirty-minute) interviews with four to five lawyers from the firm, plus a social outing such as lunch or dinner.

Typically, lawyers sent by firms to interview law students during the annual on-campus recruiting process have at least one thing in common, besides having a JD: they don't remember what it was like to be on the other side of the table as a first-year or second-year law student. They also tend to forget that they themselves usually had very little idea what type of law they wanted to practice after graduation (and still don't, in some cases). For you, the law student, this is not good.

Like most of my classmates, by the end of the OCI process in my 2L year, I had finally *started* to figure out my story and had a *slightly* better idea of what interviewers were actually looking for. The obvious problem was that by that point, OCI was over and I wasn't going to get a chance for a "do-over" with some of the law firms that I was most interested in.

Despite receiving an offer from the firm where I worked my 2L summer, I decided to participate in the OCI process again as a 3L. And let me tell you, I really had my story down pat by the time I was done going through the process a second time. This time I received—and accepted—an offer to join Sullivan & Cromwell LLP in New York City as a first-year associate.

Key ingredients: *If you cannot convey a compelling story about why you went to law school and what you want to do after graduating, you will probably not fare very well in the process (unless you have outstanding grades, which admittedly may be all that you need to receive an offer from many firms). However, it's not too hard to stand out from your peers simply by figuring out your story and then continuing to refine it as you go along.*

My simple solution for interview success is **creating your own cohesive story** about (i) why you went to law school, (ii) what your future plans are, and (iii) how a particular employer fits into those plans. But there's more to it than that, as an interviewer never starts out an interview by asking "what's your story" and then gives you the next twenty minutes to respond. I believe that the key to effectively communicating your story is to create three or four talking points* and then—much like a politician during a debate—relating most of your answers back to one of your main points or themes from your story in as natural a way as possible. For example, if you are from the East Coast or at an East Coast school but interviewing with West Coast firms, one talking point should definitely explain your interest in relocating after graduation. The interviewers will want to know, and it's much better to address this directly as part of your story than waiting for them to bring it up themselves.

PUTTING IT INTO PRACTICE

What might this look like in an actual interview? Let's say you worked for a bank before law school. A basic narrative is that you really enjoyed learning about the bank's operations, but found that you were actually most interested in the legal challenges facing the banking industry, making time to read up on these issues at night even after putting in long hours at work. So, you decided to go to law school. Then, during your

* It is critical to be genuine and authentic when developing your talking points—use of the word "story" in this section does not mean inventing any sort of fictional narrative about your background, experience, or interests. Much like your resume, these talking points will need to be adapted to your audience, as you will naturally want to emphasize elements of your journey that are most relevant to the particular individual and/or organization you are interviewing with.

1L summer you had a chance to work for the U.S. Securities and Exchange Commission in Washington, D.C. You're now looking to work at a firm with clients in the banking industry so that you can use your banking background to help inform your legal practice and provide excellent client service since you will have a better idea of how the client's business or industry actually works.

Based on this scenario, your main talking points for your interviews might be: (i) you understand the business needs of the clients that the firm has; (ii) you're used to working long hours as a junior person at a company; and (iii) you know that after graduating you want to work at a firm that has an active practice with clients in the financial industry in order to build on all of your past experiences.

If this was your profile and you were asked what your favorite course was during your first year of law school, you might respond:

"Contracts, because I already had exposure to contracts during my work at the bank before law school, and I'm really interested in having an opportunity to see how agreements are structured as a summer associate. Now that I can take electives, I also look forward to being able to take a course on Securities Regulation during my second year of law school. Taking this course will allow me to learn about some of the most important laws facing financial companies, like Dodd–Frank and the 1934 Act, which I know will be critical for being able to advise clients in this industry, and that

I already had some exposure to over the summer while working at the Securities and Exchange Commission."

It's okay if you don't have an obvious common thread for all of your past experiences. I certainly didn't. To tie it all together, I told a story about following the advice of several burned-out lawyers who all told me to take time off to explore other interests before going to law school. I spoke about taking their advice and trying out politics and starting my own company. I also emphasized that after trying those paths, I still wanted to go to law school and become a lawyer. I talked about seeing how, during my 1L summer working at the Department of Justice, antitrust lawyers actually learn a lot about business. Finally, I spoke about wanting to be an antitrust lawyer (or a general commercial litigator) after law school so that I could combine my interests in law and business. In short, I was able to tell a compelling story about why I wanted to work at a big firm, even though someone just looking at my resume might wonder why—or if—I actually wanted to be a lawyer. The key is to focus on telling a **genuine** story that is consistent with your background and interests and that relates to work which that particular firm actually does.

Pro tip: *To help you get started on thinking about your potential talking points, check out my list of the top ten most common questions interviewers ask, which follows this section. Don't forget to practice answering these questions*

***out loud**! The actual interview should not be the first time you are hearing how your answers to these common questions sound. Attend mock interview sessions, practice with friends—do anything you can to feel comfortable responding before you sit down for your interviews.*

THE BOTTOM LINE: Interviewing is more art than science, and luck can certainly play a role in the whole process. For that reason, there's no magic formula to any of this. But I do strongly believe that taking the time to be prepared and strategic about how you tell your story can make a world of difference in helping you stand out from other candidates. When you combine that with some old-fashioned hard work, like doing your due diligence on potential employers, and show gratitude and attention to detail by sending thank-you notes, I think you will be putting yourself in the best position possible to land a great job.

TOP TEN INTERVIEW QUESTIONS

Visit the Surthriving Law website to download a free copy of these questions.

Based on my experience, these are the top ten questions you must be prepared to answer confidently and competently in an interview for an associate position with a law firm. Remember that interviewers want to learn about *you* and your experiences. As one partner from Kirkland and Ellis put it: "The interviews I find most interesting and impactful tend to be those where the student discusses a specific anecdote from his or her personal experience in a complex problem they faced in a school environment and how they solved it. Something to explain how they go through their work process and are skilled at solving problems or why it is they might be interested in the practice of law. That personal experience and touch ... those are the things that are most memorable."[35]

Refer back to the tips in this chapter to help you thoughtfully craft your story so you can apply it within the context of these questions.

TOP 10 QUESTIONS YOU MUST BE PREPARED TO ANSWER DURING LAW FIRM INTERVIEWS

1. Could you tell me a little about yourself?
   This opening question is inviting you to (concisely) share your story. Be ready with your key talking points!

   ____

   ____

   ____

2. Tell me about your job/work/internship this summer. What was an interesting project that you worked on?

   ____

   ____

   ____

3. What was your favorite class during your first year of law school? Why?

   ____

   ____

   ____

4. What do you know about our firm and/or what interests you about our firm?
   Don't forget to connect your story to work being done by that particular firm or organization.

   ____

   ____

   ____

5. Why do you want to practice in this specific office/location? *This is sometimes followed up with: Are you considering any other locations?*

____

____

____

6. Are you more interested in doing corporate or litigation work? Why?

____

____

____

7. Why did you do [fill in the blank from your resume] before you went to law school?

____

____

____

8. What is your favorite part about law school so far?

____

____

____

9. What are your interests outside of law school?

____

____

____

10. Where do you see yourself five years from now?

____

____

____

*Bonus question (*if applicable*): Can you tell me more about the topic of your journal note?

____

____

____

Chapter 11

THE NEXT ROUND

After you have made it past the first round of any interview process, you have even more research and due diligence to do on your potential employer. While this section focuses primarily on callback interviews for large law firms, there are several broadly applicable takeaways, namely: know your audience, know your story, and make a connection.

Law firm callback interviews differ from on-campus "screeners" in several notable ways. Many of the existing articles on this subject offer tip after tip without presenting an overarching strategy to help prepare students for their callbacks or any other type of follow-up interview, even for smaller firms outside of BigLaw where many start their legal careers.

This section covers key differences between these interview rounds, and provides a three-step outline for achieving success in callback interviews and ultimately landing a coveted offer from a great firm. For anyone wanting to skip straight to the bottom line, I believe the key to success in callbacks is: (i) doing background research on the firm generally, and on the office/interviewers specifically; (ii) proactively incorporating this information into a cohesive narrative about why you are interested in that particular firm and office; and (iii) trying to make a connection with everyone you meet with during the course of your interviews.

Quick tip: *At the end of this chapter is a template I created to help you structure your pre-interview research process. This form also includes a section for jotting down one to three memorable things about each person that you meet with during the course of your interviews. These thoughts can be helpful when writing thank-you notes and for making decisions if you have multiple offers.*

WHY DO CALLBACKS?

Being invited to a callback generally means you are seen as qualified and potentially capable of joining the firm as a first-year associate by the lawyer who interviewed you. While this is certainly an achievement, it's not enough to ensure an actual offer from a firm. Because the on-campus interview process is so truncated, law firms use callbacks to spend more time attempting to determine if you are a good fit for that particular office. In my opinion, the whole process is highly inefficient, but I'll save the editorial on that for a different forum.

Your callback interviewers are generally trying to figure out two things: (i) whether you will be interested in the type of work and clients that generally keep associates in that office busy, hence making it more likely that you will stick around for an appreciable period of time rather than jumping ship at the earliest possible opportunity; and (ii) if you will be a good cultural fit for the office. This includes everything from whether they like you on a personal level, to whether they think you can handle the workload and stress, to your perceived ability to interact professionally with others ranging from clients, co-workers, and support staff. Be sure to keep both of these points in mind as you prepare for your callback.

Quick point: *You might be surprised by the lack of time and effort that many firms spend training their attorneys on how to conduct effective interviews. As a result, most callback candidates are faced with unstructured interviews that are inherently subjective. There is a great deal of research indicating that these types of interviews are not very good* *predictors of success and that they introduce the potential for a great deal of bias.*[36] *Nevertheless, these interviews unfortunately don't seem to be going away anytime soon, although perhaps this might change in the future. For now, this means that you will still be faced with—and need to be prepared for—a wide range of different interview styles, and should make an effort to effectively manage impressions formed by your interviewers. You unfortunately may also experience some very awkward or unprofessional situations. The one that sticks out for me was an associate who told me mid-callback that "it would be a mistake to put this firm's name on your resume." Always stay calm, collected, and poised, regardless of the circumstances.*

There are two main types of differences that typically distinguish callback interviews from on-campus interviews; one type is structural while the other is philosophical. Understanding these differences will help you better prepare for callbacks.

Structural differences include an extra ten minutes for each callback interview at the law firm (thirty minutes versus twenty minutes for the typical on-campus interview); four to five interviews without a break (the typical OCI schedule has breaks in between your interviews with different firms); and a social outing (lunch or dinner). This gives you more time to make a connection with your interviewers, which is a good thing, as we'll see in Step 3 in the following pages. It also means that you will need to spend more time thinking of potential questions in case you need to carry the conversation.

Philosophical differences refer to the fact that for a callback interview someone (usually a committee) at the firm has already determined that your competence and qualifications exceed a specific threshold needed to potentially be hired. Your on-campus interviewer(s) have vouched for you, and said they think it is worth the time and expense of having others at the firm meet you. This should give you at least a bit of confidence heading into your callback interviews.

Quick tip: *Don't forget that a callback is also your chance to evaluate the firm as a potential employer. It is important to use that opportunity to ask specific questions about the type of work you are interested in, and to learn more about the people (potentially your future colleagues) who work in that particular office.*

THE STRATEGY

In an effort to once again go beyond the basics of Interviewing 101, here is a strategy, composed of three parts, that I recommend focusing on when preparing for a callback or follow-up interview: know your audience, know your story, and make a connection.

Quick point: *You should certainly not ignore basic advice like getting a good night's sleep before your callback, arriving (or in the case of a video conference, signing in) early, being polite, dressing professionally, etcetera. I am treating all of those points as a given, and focusing on the things I believe can give you an edge compared to other similarly situated candidates.*

STEP 1: KNOW YOUR AUDIENCE

Anyone who has played competitive sports knows that your strategy varies depending on who you are up against. Your likelihood of success is often determined by your ability to adapt your play to the unique characteristics of a given opponent. This requires doing your homework to learn more about them, as this allows you to change your approach and maximize your probability of success.

While obviously not a perfect analogy, it is important to realize that the questions you ask and points you emphasize during your callback should similarly be tailored to the person sitting across the table (or screen) from you. For that reason, you should think strategically about the different types of lawyers that you are likely to encounter at your next callback.

Recruiting departments usually try to include a mix of seniority levels on your callback schedule, namely: partners, mid-to-senior associates, and junior associates. Each of these groups is likely to have a different perspective based on their current role at the firm, their practice group, and their work experience.

Pro tip: *The recruiting and support staff are a vital part of each firm. Everyone you encounter during the course of your day should always be treated with the utmost respect and professionalism. You should assume that their feedback will be taken into account by the recruiting committee, and any reports of candidates being disrespectful to anyone at the firm will almost certainly result in a "no offer" situation.*

Partners: Partners have the most invested in the firm of anyone on your callback schedule. They have been at the firm the longest, and, if they are an equity partner, they own part of the company. They have often spent significant amounts of time and money developing client relationships, and the associates they hire will reflect not just on the firm generally, but on them personally. They are also the furthest removed from law school, and may have forgotten what it's like to be in your shoes trying to make career decisions after just one year of law school. I recommend focusing your questions for partners on "bigger picture" questions, like what skills helped them become partners, traits of the most successful associates, how the firm or office has changed over time, questions about different practice groups, and the extent to which associates are involved in business development. In other words, make an effort to demonstrate an interest in a long-term future at the firm. You should also pay special attention to whether a partner on your schedule is the head of the office or of an important firm committee, or holds another specific role. You demonstrate attention to detail and a real interest in the company by asking questions about the partner's leadership role, which can go a long way in differentiating you from other candidates who didn't bother looking up or asking about that information.

Mid-to-Senior Associates: These more senior associates often have to help run cases or deals for the partners they work for. While some may be on the "partnership track," others may not be taking this route. Their primary concern is often whether you can handle the workload and work well with others on a team. You may want to focus on asking them questions about how cases are staffed, how assignments are given, and opportunities for junior associates. Providing concrete examples of situations where you have been able to work long hours or under pressure for extended periods of time is likely to resonate with these associates. Given that they have spent five or more years at the firm, these associates may also be well positioned to share their perspective on work–life balance with you.

Junior Associates: These lawyers are the most recent additions to the firm and the people you would most likely go with on a coffee run if you end up working at the firm. They are still learning the ropes, figuring out how things work, and cultivating relationships with more senior lawyers. Your conversations with junior associates can be less formal (junior associates often go on the lunch interviews), and are often the most helpful for understanding the types of cases and work that you would be given as a first-year associate. However, they still submit reviews, so don't let your guard down too much!

Know the firm and office: Another very important aspect of knowing your audience is researching the firm generally, as well as specifics about the office and everyone on your callback schedule. While this falls into the more traditional advice for callbacks, it bears repeating because it is absolutely critical. For example, one partner at Kirkland & Ellis specifically noted that a major "pet peeve" is when people "come in and don't know anything about the firm."[37] If you are serious about getting an offer, then you must spend time doing research on Google, LinkedIn, NALP (National Association for Law Placement), as well as the firm's own website. While most large law firms represent large corporate clients, they each have cases, clients, and matters unique to the firm and office. It is your job to find matters they have handled that you think would be interesting to work on and relate that back to your background or interests, as we'll explore in the next section. Don't forget to ask for help from 3Ls at your school, alumni, or anyone else with a connection to someone who currently works at the firm. Any insight you can get will certainly help you to stand out from the crowd.

STEP 2: KNOW YOUR STORY

You will almost certainly encounter a range of interview styles during the OCI and callback interview process. Some interviewers are more freewheeling, while others methodically go through your resume bullet point by bullet point. But one commonality, whether stated or not, is that interviewers want to know if you actually want to work at their firm, in their specific office and city. As discussed earlier, by the callback stage you have already been vetted and deemed capable and intelligent by the firm that has called you in for office interviews. However, it's safe to assume that each interviewer will still want to understand where you're coming from and where you're going—or at least what your best guess is at this point in time. This will often come up in the context of whether you are more interested in the firm's corporate or litigation department.

How do you prepare for this line of questioning? In my experience, the best thing to do is proactively develop a short, cohesive, and genuine narrative tying together your background and interest in practicing law generally with your specific interest in working for this firm, in this particular office. This is why it is so important to do your homework, as it will help you develop a story that demonstrates an authentic interest that is obvious to everyone on your interview schedule.

This is also a good opportunity to utilize your talking points that were suggested in the previous chapter. Just be sure that you thoughtfully tailor these points based on your audience. By doing this, you will come across as poised and confident, and as someone who is ready to hit the ground running. A well-constructed narrative also helps eliminate questions when the recruiting committee meets to determine if you are really interested in working at their firm.

STEP 3: MAKE A CONNECTION

One of the best ways to stand out from other applicants is by having a memorable conversation with your interviewer; in other words, making a connection. This usually happens when you are engaged in an active dialogue with your interviewer, asking them questions about their work, and what they like doing outside the office (hint: look for clues about favorite sports, teams, and interests as you walk into their office). This makes intuitive sense, and is reflected in books like Dale Carnegie's *How to Win Friends and Influence People* (which I recommend as a quick and helpful read).

This is an area that can be particularly challenging or intimidating if you don't share a similar background or profile as the person interviewing you. In those situations, I always try to find something more general that we can relate to and connect on. Things like food or music or television shows often work well as icebreakers. For example, when interviewing with New York firms, I would often ask interviewers about their favorite pizza places in NYC, as it seems like everyone has an opinion. It also gave me a chance to talk about my knowledge of the city despite the fact I didn't have much of a connection to it.

Given that callback interviews usually run thirty minutes long, there is ample time, particularly at the beginning and end of the interview, for you to spend a few minutes (or more) building rapport with your interviewer. The more that you have bonded over some topic of conversation—whether academic, professional, or recreational—the more likely it is that you will get a high score from the interviewer when they submit their evaluation to the recruiting department.

Pro tip: *Make sure to be fully present, engaged, and listening—even if it's your last interview at the end of a* *long day. At many firms, it only takes one person on your interview schedule giving you a mediocre review to tank your chances of getting an offer.*

THE BOTTOM LINE: After making it through on-campus interviews, getting a callback is the final audition for a lucrative job as a first-year associate. Like any audition, your odds of landing the role are highly dependent on how much you prepare, and how well you execute your performance. While you can't control every variable, you can do your homework on the firm, and think about how your interest in that specific office fits into a broader narrative about your own background and experience. Finally, don't forget to focus on finding common ground with each interviewer. The more allies advocating for you to get an offer at the weekly recruiting/hiring committee meeting, the better. Good luck!

INTERVIEW PREPARATION WORKSHEET

Visit the Surthriving Law website to download a free copy of this worksheet.

Firm Name: ______________________________

Date of Interview: ______________________________

BACKGROUND INFORMATION – OFFICE OF INTERVIEW

Office/City: ______________________________

Managing Partner (office): ______________________________

Head of Recruiting (office): ______________________________

Attorney(s) for 1st Round/OCI: ______________________________

Recent cases in news (office): ______________________________

____

____

Number of Lawyers (office): ______________________________

BACKGROUND INFORMATION – NATIONAL (IF APPLICABLE)

Managing Partner (firmwide): ______________________________

Head of Recruiting (firmwide): ______________________________

Recent cases in news (firmwide): ______________________________

____

____

Number of Offices (total): ______________________________

Number of Lawyers (total): ______________________________

BACKGROUND INFORMATION – INTERVIEWER PANEL/SCHEDULE

	#1	#2	#3
Name			
Position			
Class/Grad Year			
Undergrad School			
Law School			
Notes from Bio			
Date of Thank You Email			

	#4	#5	#6
Name			
Position			
Class/Grad Year			
Undergrad School			
Law School			
Notes from Bio			
Date of Thank You Email			

MEMORABLE NOTES

List one to three memorable points or stories from each of your interviews.

Chapter 12

VIRTUAL INTERVIEWING

Even before the pandemic, interviewing was being conducted over video conferencing technology. This trend has accelerated due to current limitations around in-person, indoor meeting spaces. While much of the previous advice is applicable regardless of technology, certain things are worth being mindful of when you are not able to be in the same room as your interviewer.

As mentioned earlier, the impacts of the COVID-19 pandemic have caused many changes in business processes, including how interviews are conducted.[38] Virtual interviews have become much more common, and may remain so as we move forward. Here are a few notable things that I have observed in virtual interviews myself—as both an interviewer and interviewee—over the past twelve to eighteen months.

TEST THE TECHNOLOGY

Starting with the basics, it is absolutely critical to know and test whatever type of video conferencing software you are using *before* you log in for your interview. Sounds obvious, right? Let me tell you what's even more obvious: when you're interviewing someone who clearly hasn't taken the time to do this prior to the interview. Even if you are familiar with the platform, still take the time to do a trial run to make sure things like your background and screen name defaults are appropriate for a business setting. And definitely log into your interview with plenty of time to spare in case you need to do any last minute troubleshooting.

Several interviews for my current role were conducted remotely over Google Meet. I had never used the platform before, nor did I have a webcam. I invested in a decent one and made sure my home WiFi service had enough bandwidth for a good connection well in advance of the interviews. The goal here is to have everything go seamlessly on the technology side so that 100% of your energy can go into concentrating on the interview and your interviewer.

BE PREPARED FOR SOMETHING TO GO WRONG

Even after following the above advice, you still need a backup plan if (okay, *when*) something goes wrong. Inevitably, something will happen. Be prepared to offer solutions. For example, if the video quality suddenly goes downhill for more than a minute or two, you can offer to switch off cameras to try and conserve bandwidth—this might even be a relief for your interviewer, especially if it's early in the morning or late in their day! You can also offer to drop off of the video conference entirely and call them directly. It might be less high tech, but you will probably be positioned to have a better, less distracted conversation that way.

Pivoting quickly to a backup option demonstrates to your interviewer that you're able to stay poised and calm in a stressful situation. It will also show that you're well prepared to successfully manage similar real world situations that have become quite common for most professionals in the pandemic era. No matter what happens, the most important thing to do is to stay in touch with your recruiting contact. If you do have tech issues, you should have their contact information handy so that you can immediately call or email them. The absolute worst thing that you can do is be a no-show and fail to communicate in real time about what's happening.

KEEP YOUR ENERGY HIGH AND STAY ENGAGED

Finally, be sure not to let interviewing basics like maintaining good energy and eye contact go out the window just because you happen to be sitting in your kitchen or bedroom for the interview. If you are looking down at notes, come across as distracted, disinterested, or disengaged, or otherwise don't stay fully present, you can lose your audience even more quickly over a video conference than in person. It's important to remember there's an actual person on the other side of the screen. If they have something prominent in their background (such as an interesting piece of artwork) that catches your attention, ask them about it with genuine interest. This includes unexpected cameos by children, pets, and significant others. Creating a strong connection with your virtual interviewer is just as important, if not more so, as when you are in the same space together.

THE BOTTOM LINE: Although I haven't done nearly as much remote interviewing compared to in-person, I have still learned a few important lessons. First, all of the previous interviewing advice holds true in terms of preparation and research on the potential employer and your interviewers. During your interviews, it is still important to pay attention to visual cues that might tell you more about your interviewer. Are they using a default background of a beach or fancy mansion? If so, it's probably worth spending a minute or two exploring that with curiosity and interest. Finally, make sure to spend extra time preparing for the technology and logistics, including a contingency plan if you run into tech issues. It will be worth the time when you can spend the interview focused on creating a strong connection with the person interviewing you, versus solving problems with your actual internet connection.

Chapter 13

ACCEPTING AN OFFER: IT'S NOT ALWAYS EASY

After investing a significant amount of time and bandwidth on your job search, your efforts will all pay off—I promise! But getting an offer does not mean you should always accept it, as hard as that might be in some cases. This section provides considerations for you to take into account before saying "I do" and signing on the dotted line. This advice also extends to efforts by your current employer to retain you.

You've made it through the entire interview process. It's fantastic that you've gotten an offer, and even more so if you are in the enviable position of having multiple offers to consider. But even though you have made it through the frenzy of interviews, seemingly endless small talk, and possibly even a flight, the final step often feels like the most difficult part of the entire process. This section attempts to provide clarity and guidance for anyone currently faced with making this important decision about what offer to accept.

IS IT REALLY *THAT* IMPORTANT?

While some people may downplay the significance of this decision for a variety of reasons (most likely as a way to try to help alleviate your anxiety), I tend to disagree. The truth is that yes, this *is* a big deal. As we know, law school is a major investment of your time and money, and the firm that you pick now will be on your resume for years to come. More importantly, this firm will serve as a foundation for the professional brand you are starting to build as a new lawyer; for those of you transitioning from another career, it will be a key part of your professional evolution. It is certainly worth taking time to reflect—but not stress—about this decision so that you continue to feel confident after you have actually accepted an offer.

Quick point: *For anyone deciding between multiple offers, it is imperative to be grateful, humble, and mindful that many of your classmates may not have fared as well as you did in the interview process, while others may have opted for a* *completely different career path altogether. Be considerate and respectful of the experiences of others.*

HOW DO I DECIDE?

The single most important factor, as drawn from my experience and informal conversations with many others in your position, is a highly subjective one: How does the *idea* of working at each firm make you feel when you think about it? Your gut reaction to this question is a result of the subconscious processing of a number of data points from the many interactions that you have had along the way with individuals at each of these firms. This includes everything from your correspondence with the recruiting department, to the many conversations with partners and associates, to the physical office space and location of each firm.

Quick tip: *Hopefully you have been jotting down notes immediately after each of your interviews on the worksheet provided in Chapter 11. These notes will be quite useful for refreshing your recollections long after the interviews are over.*

In my experience, there is typically one firm that feels like a particularly good fit, one in which you had a number of memorable conversations, and where people enthusiastically reached out to you after the offer was extended—you feel genuinely excited about the prospect of working there. This is more than likely the best firm for you, even if it isn't rated highest on the Am Law 100 report. On the other hand, there is probably at least one firm where you experienced an awkward, uncomfortable, or even inappropriate exchange that can now be crossed off your list of potential employers.

IT'S NOT THAT SIMPLE, IS IT?

No, gut feeling alone probably isn't going to be outcome determinative for you given the significance of this decision. There are at least two other important considerations to take into account: I call them "career narrative" and "network opinion."

CAREER NARRATIVE

There is a strong likelihood that you will not be working at whatever firm you pick for your entire legal career. This means you should already be thinking about what your story will be when you are applying to potential employers down the road. While it can be difficult to envision where you'll be three to five years from now, the exercise is still an important one to go through *before* you make your initial decision. For example, if your long-term goal is going "in-house" as a labor and employment attorney, then you probably should not accept an offer from a firm that is primarily focused on doing securities work. Even if you're not sure which type of law you will ultimately end up practicing, which is certainly the case for many law students, you can see if the firm handles matters for clients that you'd like to work for.

The key point here is that just because a firm is ranked higher on the Am Law 100 report or the Vault Law 100 report, it does not automatically mean it is a better career choice for you. If there is a particular partner or group that you're interested in at a smaller or less well-known firm, that is also very important to take into account for your future plans. You will be happier and do better work in an environment surrounded by people you like and get along with, while working on the types of matters that interest you. Depending on your career goals, BigLaw may not even be the best starting point for you.

Quick point: *There may be certain situations (like wanting to be an Assistant U.S. Attorney or a federal judge) where the prestige of the firm that you choose really does make a significant difference. The suggestion here is that rankings should not be the sole thing guiding your decision.*

NETWORK OPINION

Your friends, family, and professional connections can also play an important role in the decision-making process. These are people who may know more about a given firm's reputation or even know someone currently employed by the firm who can give you a candid assessment of what it is like to actually work there. These conversations can be particularly informative, and help validate your general feelings regarding the firm. If you can't find anyone through your personal contacts, you can always use LinkedIn or your law school's Career Services office to find alumni who work at the firms on your short list. You can also contact the recruiting department for each firm and ask if there is someone available to speak with you, e.g., "I'm interested in speaking with more junior litigation associates to learn more about their work at the firm before making a final decision." Most firms are more than willing to accommodate this type of request, and their reaction to your queries may also help guide you in the decision-making process.

Pro tip: *Remember that many 3Ls at your school just completed their work as summer associates at firms you may be considering. It is definitely worth contacting them to discuss their experience and for help with additional introductions to associates or partners they worked with over the summer.*

THE BOTTOM LINE: There are many factors that go into determining what offer you will ultimately accept. No algorithm, formula, or AI exists (at least at the moment) to make this decision easy for you. Because of that, it is important to reflect on *all* of your experiences to see which firm is the best fit for you. It is also worth spending time thinking about how each firm fits into your longer-term career plan, and what others in your network think of the "finalists" on your list. While this is a significant decision, remember that it is not a permanent one. So go ahead and call the hiring partner of whatever firm you think is the right choice for you—they'll be happy to hear from you!

Part IV

LIFE AFTER LAW SCHOOL

TIME TO PRACTICE (LAW, THAT IS!)

Well, the good news is that you finally graduated and have accepted a position. Congratulations! After all of that hard work taking the LSAT, applying to law school, and then spending three years actually going to law school and finding a job, now you can **start** *your legal career. Well, almost. First, you need to pass the bar exam. And once that is behind you, then you get to learn the ropes of what it takes to actually practice law for a living, not just study it. Long story short: You still have plenty to look forward to on your career journey in law.*

My own career path has been filled with a number of twists, turns, and detours. I hope my own experiences—everything from changing offices (and coasts) and law firms to going in-house—will help provide you with insight and perspective as you ponder whether to make similar choices yourself. This includes questions like "How much different would it be at another firm?" (probably not as much as you'd like), and "How much better is in-house?" (a lot if you ask me!).

But as you will note, there are plenty of things I haven't done, and experiences in law that I have not had. For example, I have never made partner at a law firm, held a full-time clerkship, or spent my career in public interest law. Fortunately, a number of guest contributors who do have these professional experiences have generously agreed to share their unique perspectives and insights in Parts V and VI. For now, I hope that you still find a great deal of value from my own advice based on the experiences that I have had.

Career Context: *Here is a look at the rest of my legal journey on the career front, from graduation to law firms to a secondment to going in-house. Never a dull moment!*

MY POST-GRADUATION EXPERIENCE (IN A NUTSHELL):

- Summer post-graduation: Studied for New York bar exam (Chicago and New York).
- Litigation Associate at Sullivan & Cromwell LLP (New York, NY).
- Litigation Associate at Sullivan & Cromwell (Los Angeles, CA).
- Litigation Associate & Counsel at O'Melveny & Myers LLP (Los Angeles, CA).
- Secondment at Sony Pictures (Culver City, CA).
- In-house counsel at Sony Pictures (Culver City, CA).
- In-house counsel at another global entertainment company (Los Angeles, CA).

Chapter 14

TAKING THE BAR EXAM

After taking and passing the California and New York bar exams, I can attest to the fact that no bar exam is my idea of a good time. But I did find that being disciplined about studying daily and still fitting in time for fun and creating outlets for stress (like a summer beach volleyball league) really helped make the whole experience less unpleasant. After the exam is over, focus only on what you can control, and avoid unnecessary stress about things you can't—like the grading of your exam—as that's in someone else's hands.

Studying for the bar exam was not a particularly fun experience for me (or pretty much anyone from what I hear). I took—and passed—my first bar exam (New York) after spending the summer after law school graduation diligently taking a costly bar exam prep course that the law firm I was going to work for thankfully covered. Years later I would take—and pass—my second bar exam (California) with just a week off work to study for the exam, and using old exam prep materials I borrowed from a friend.

In my experience, the single best thing you can do to prepare for the bar exam is to develop a study/prep ritual. Using tools from the surthrival toolbox covered in Part I will definitely help you on that front, particularly in creating a study schedule and sticking to it. The people that I've seen struggle the most with bar exam prep are the ones who didn't put in time *every* day making steady progress and instead tried to cram everything in when it was much too late in the game. The key point here is to focus on what's under your control each day (studying), versus worrying about the outcome of the exam that you haven't even taken yet. This is the type of thinking that is aligned with the Stoicism principles we looked at in the surthrival toolbox.

You also want—I would say *need*—to schedule time for *not* studying. Not a ton of time, but enough to still relax, unwind, and have fun. For me, this was a summer beach volleyball league along the shores of Lake Michigan in Chicago. Don't fall into the "I just" trap that I described at the very beginning of this guide and lock yourself into a room for the entire summer until it's time for the exam.

Once you have finished taking the bar, I highly recommend that you **assume that you passed**. If you adopt this mindset, you won't spend time comparing questions and answers with anyone after it's over, or worrying yourself sick that you failed one of the essays. The outcome is totally outside of your control at this point, and the more you can embrace and accept that reality, the better. If you later find out that you unfortunately didn't pass, you can deal with it then. No amount of worrying about the results before you know them will help you. To the contrary, you will be wasting valuable time and energy that could be spent living your life before starting your first job after law school. For me, this was one of the last times that I can remember where there was nothing that I *had* to do. So relax and take a trip (or at least a breather) if there's any way you possibly can!

THE BOTTOM LINE: Even if no one particularly enjoys studying for the bar exam after graduating from law school, your experience is entirely up to you. Signing up for a bar exam prep course from an established company and keeping up with all of the assigned material is critical. Using the surthrival tools from Part I, you can take a focused approach to creating healthy study rituals that will still give you time to prioritize health, wellness, and even some fun in between your planned study sessions. Don't fall into the trap of "I just" thinking and put everything else that's important to you on hold for an exam. Prioritize both studying *and* having fun, but don't overdo it with either of them. Once you have finally finished taking the bar (yay!), do everything that you possibly can to relax, unwind, and take a break—especially if you're about to start your legal career working at a law firm. Trust me on this one!

Chapter 15

THE FIRM

Much has been written about law firm life, both fiction and non-fiction. In this section I focus on a specific set of insights on how to navigate firm life based on my own experience working at several large law firms.

Law firms come in all shapes and sizes. Although I worked at smaller law firms before law school, as a practicing lawyer I started my career working at large law firms. Because all firms are different, and because many law students will go on to work at smaller firms, I will try to keep this section focused on advice that is more broadly relevant to a variety of firms. Note that you can also read more about my experiences working at large law firms in the appendix.

Let's start with a basic principle. When clients are billed solely or at least mostly based on how many hours—or tenths of an hour—that you work, your employer (the firm) has a very strong financial incentive to ensure that you are keeping busy billing clients, i.e., that you are working. The path then to increasing the amount of profits for partners (and thus the amount available to compensate associates) at firms is pretty straightforward. Profits only increase when (i) rates increase, (ii) hours billed increase, or (iii) both. Firms tend not to increase hourly rates more than once a year (at most), especially as competition for business increases and there is no shortage of lawyers on the horizon (at least in the United States). As such, the single best—and sometimes only—lever for firms to pull regarding profit is more billable hours.

Why does this matter to you? It means that it's up to you and *only* you to prioritize self-care and create healthy (or at least less unhealthy) work practices, because unfortunately, the owners of the law firms—the partners—don't have a strong financial incentive for anyone at the firm to bill fewer hours. While there has generally been more talk in the field of law about the importance of health and wellness in firms, only you really know how burned out you're feeling at any given point in time.

Speaking of burnout, it's real. If you happen to be someone who generally tries really hard, is a high performer, wants to excel professionally, and/or has student loans you are trying to pay off (here's looking at you, reader), then you're probably going to put quite a bit of pressure on yourself to do well at work. And that's even without a partner breathing down your neck for a memo! As you'll see when we get to the next topic on changing law firms, many of these fundamentals—namely, how firms make money and how you are internally motivated—do not change regardless of which firm you're working for or what type of law you practice. This is another reason why it's helpful to have worked at a law firm before you decide to go to law school. Sometimes it takes the firsthand experience of working alongside lawyers as a paralegal to realize that working at a firm might not be all that it's cracked up to be.

The power of no (or "yes, and"): *One of the hardest things for me as a junior associate was saying "no" to assignments. A million thoughts and concerns would race through my mind, most of which I never bothered raising with the person assigning me more work. If you're starting to feel overloaded, try to lean in and be candid with the person giving you the assignment. It's much better for a partner or senior associate to hear "I'd love to help but need to get a depo outline finished by tomorrow morning. Is there someone else who can take this one?" than it is to push yourself, stay up all night, and then potentially deliver a sub-optimal work product at the expense of your mental and physical well-being. To borrow a trick from the improv world (previously discussed in Chapter 8), you can also try saying* *"yes, and…." For example: "**Yes**, I'd love to help on that **and** I have a depo outline to finish by tomorrow morning. Is this something that I can get started on later this week?" You'll never know unless you ask, and by framing it positively your response should hopefully be well received.*

Aside from setting your own boundaries—or at least trying to—and using the tools from the surthrival toolbox, what else can you do to surthrive firm life? As you are starting out at the firm, I think the most important thing to do is focus on building **strong relationships with partners** who are willing to take you under their wing. Ideally, this would be someone working in a practice area of interest to you. As you start to build those types of relationships, you can be proactive about seeking mentoring advice and professional development opportunities. This mentor relationship also has the benefit of giving you an ally to help shield you from other assignments or people that you might prefer to avoid. Even if your firm has an official mentoring program, use any opportunities you can to directly connect with people who can provide you with mentorship and guide you on your journey. These types of relationships can truly be game-changers in your career at the firm—and even down the road!

THE BOTTOM LINE: Work–life balance is fundamentally difficult in an environment where highly motivated people have compensation and promotion opportunities that are deeply connected to the number of their billable hours. Well-being has historically not been prioritized by the owners of law firms (partners) in part due to the direct financial impact when associates spend time away from billing for any reason (whether self-care, vacations, or simply sleep). Because this leads to burnout, it's up to you to manage your own health and well-being. One potentially helpful way to keep from getting overwhelmed is finding a partner at the firm who models more balanced lifestyle choices and who can help mentor and guide you as you navigate these challenges yourself.

Chapter 16
LATERALING

It often doesn't take long before associates start wondering what life might be like if they moved to another law firm. Surely things must be different, you might think. The people are different. The clients are different. While true, I've found there are more similarities than differences, which is primarily due to the nature of the work itself (contracts are still contracts, litigation is still litigation), and the billable hours. I've found the key is to really reflect on why you're thinking about changing firms and if a new firm can truly help you accomplish those goals.

Once you have been working at a law firm for some time, it's not uncommon to start wondering if the grass might be greener at a different one. You've now gotten to know and work with a few of the partners and associates. Maybe you've had a few too many late work nights, or maybe you don't feel valued for your contributions. You might start feeling like there is something left to be desired from the entire experience. Surely other firms out there must not have quite the same mix of challenging personalities, long hours, and less than stimulating work, right? Once you start to have these thoughts, my experience is that they don't go away. So what do you do about them?

After four years of working for a large New York-based law firm (first in the NYC office and later in a Southern California office), I decided to make a lateral move to a large Los Angeles-based law firm. This journey started after a recruiter reached out to me about an opportunity that checked all the boxes for me. The first plus was getting actual trial experience, which was a major selling point for making the change to a new firm. Second, since I was already in Los Angeles at the time, I was also very interested in working for a firm with more LA-based clients, especially in the entertainment space. And finally, after working in the California office of the New York firm, I was also interested in working in an office that had a bigger local footprint and was connected to the local legal community in Southern California.

Once I switched firms, I did get the trial experience that I had been trying to find. "Be careful what you wish for" was my main lesson there. The long hours and high stress of a jury trial was pretty intense. The new firm was also more connected to local entertainment companies in Los Angeles (more on that in the next section). Surprisingly though, I've found the firms that I've worked for over the years tend to have many more similarities than differences. As noted in the previous section, I think these similarities between firms, especially when you're talking about large, corporate law firms, are mostly due to structural concerns—billable hours, the nature of legal work, and the types of people drawn to the practice of law.

Before changing firms, the best advice I have for you is to be really clear about *why* you are making the change and *what* your goals are if you move to a new firm. Are you seeking to work with different types of clients or at a much smaller law firm? Will this new firm allow you to focus on a more specialized practice area that's not an option for you at your current firm? These are goals that a new job could help you reach. But if you are hoping to spend significantly less time working, or that the types of things you are working on every day will change, it could be a very disappointing experience. It is also worth noting the significant amount of energy and effort it takes to interview, wind down current matters, and then get onboarded into a new firm where you'll need to build new internal and external relationships. It can be a lot of work so make sure it's worth the transaction costs.

THE BOTTOM LINE: Changing law firms ("lateraling") is a decision that many practicing lawyers think about and make at some point in their careers. Beware of "the grass is always greener" type of thinking. You should also reflect on whether staying at a firm—any firm—is truly the right thing for you right now. There are certainly compelling reasons for lateraling. Maybe you want more trial experience like I did, better opportunities for making partner, or a lower billable hours requirement. Or perhaps you've realized that working in a smaller town, with a better quality of life, is actually more important to you than a bigger paycheck in a bigger and busier city. Whatever the reason(s), be realistic about the fact that you most likely will still be billing your clients by the hour and that things at the new firm might ultimately give you a sense of déjà vu.

Chapter 17

GOING IN-HOUSE

I know from personal experience that when you're ready to leave law firm life, it feels like it needs to happen immediately. In reality, trying to find an in-house role can often take six to nine months and quite a bit of patience and persistence (not the easiest things to practice when you are still working full-time at a law firm). Thankfully, there are several specific things you can do to improve your chances, including coming up with a very specific job/company/role profile so your search is more targeted and less overwhelming; developing a targeted plan for networking; and being persistent. This time is also a great opportunity to think about what you really want to do next, not just what you should do or what's most realistic.

"Luck is what happens when preparation meets opportunity."

One of the most common things I get asked about these days is how to "escape" BigLaw and land a job as in-house counsel. Whether they are an associate, counsel, or even partner, "going in-house" is (or eventually becomes) the ultimate goal for many practicing lawyers at law firms. Why? For many, the biggest selling point is the opportunity to ditch the dreaded billable hour system once and for all. These types of positions are appealing to lots of lawyers, for many different reasons, which means that open in-house roles almost always get a huge amount of highly qualified applicants for a single position. So how can you improve your chances of landing one of these highly coveted jobs given the fierce competition for them?

The above quote, often attributed* to the ancient Stoic philosopher, Seneca, really sums up the most common path to landing an in-house position. It usually takes a great deal of preparation as well as a bit of luck for lightning to strike to receive that in-house offer. As frustrating as that may sound, there are some very concrete things that you can and should do to secure an in-house role that are totally **within your control**—a very Stoic concept, by the way.

---

* My limited fact-checking didn't result in a definitive source to attribute this quote.

Need help getting started? *I've prepared a worksheet to help jump-start your preparation for finding the perfect in-house job. Check it out at the end of this chapter or on my website.*

The most important place to begin is to be as **specific as possible** when thinking about the in-house position of your dreams. What industry is it in? What city or region? What does the ideal role look like? The more specific you are, the more targeted your job search and networking conversations will be. Just imagine trying to search all of the potential job postings on LinkedIn and company job sites while *also* managing the workload of your current job. If your funnel is too wide, it will feel (and be) completely overwhelming, like looking for a job in a sea of possibilities. Taking a more targeted approach will help ensure that you're looking and applying for things that really meet your list of desires. This makes it easier for you to share genuine passion for the position and ultimately be happy in the prospective role, so there are a lot of benefits beyond just a more manageable job search process.

Articulating a very specific intention also makes it easier for others to understand what you are looking for, and how they can help you in your search. I can't emphasize the importance of this enough: those who have the clearest idea of what they're looking for next are the ones who are best able to find it by enlisting the help of others. Often when I have initial conversations with someone looking to go in-house, they don't have a very clear idea of what exactly they want, other than to leave law firm life behind for good. While this is understandable, if you aren't sure of your own goals and needs then it's that much harder for others to help you.

One great example of being mindful and intentional about approaching an in-house job search comes from an associate at a firm where I used to work in New York. This individual was focused on moving to Los Angeles and finding an in-house position similar to my own in the entertainment industry. They were able to find their dream job by using a targeted search (albeit one with plenty of preparation, networking, etcetera), ultimately landing a great in-house role at a major movie studio in Hollywood. It was the clarity of their desired career path that helped me as an advisor identify potential opportunities that might be most relevant and interesting to them.

Another example is a recent conversation I had with a current BigLaw associate. They expressed some reservations about overly focusing their job search efforts on one particular area; in this case, cryptocurrency versus finance more broadly. I explained that one big benefit of choosing a singular area of focus is that it helps demonstrate to potential employers that you have deep passion and conviction about the subject matter—that you wake up thinking about this evolving area of law, read about it, and see exactly both the state of the field as it is currently and how it could impact the potential employer's business in the future. You can then build your resume around experiences that further demonstrate your interest and expertise in this area; for example, perhaps you could publish an article or get a relevant certification before launching your job search in earnest. This can make all the difference in the world when you are trying to stand out from a highly qualified crowd of other people also looking to leave law firm life for good.

The sort of genuine enthusiasm that I'm talking about here isn't possible if you try to highlight all of the things that you *could* do, or that you've worked on many different types of matters (unless you're focused on applying for a generalist type of role, of course). Trying to keep every possibility open doesn't provide potential employers with an authentic narrative about what truly motivates you. What is that thing you feel *driven* to do next versus something that you would be just fine or okay with doing? No matter what you do, you can't fake genuine conviction. As author (and my former law school classmate) Suneel Gupta nicely puts it in his great book, *Backable*: "What moves people isn't charisma, but conviction. Backable people earnestly believe in what they're saying, and they simply let that belief shine through whatever style feels the most natural ... If you want to convince others, you must convince yourself first."[39]

Tailoring your resume: *Your resume should be tailored to tell the most genuine and authentic story about you* *for each particular position that you apply to. Make sure that when you submit your resume, each line of it reflects the best work experience you've had for that specific role. This also means making sure to review each job description carefully, and update your resume accordingly. You can also think ahead to a potential interview and questions the hiring manager might ask you. What experiences are you going to want to talk about in the interview that might not be on your "standard" or current version of your resume? As an example, maybe you have start-up experience from a long time ago that was less relevant to your current law firm role, and so it isn't on your current resume. For in-house roles, you would likely want to highlight this long-standing interest of yours on the business side of things in addition to law. Be sure to reflect on what unique work and life experiences you have had, and don't be afraid to include them on your resume. Given your career journey this far, you should have plenty of material to work with!*

There are several other important elements to a successful in-house search. Without a doubt, the most important and effective thing that you can do is to let people in your network know that you're interested in a new position and ask for their help finding it. Going back to the surthrival toolbox, this is where building a strong network of professional connections as early as possible can really be a powerful strategy to help you get to where you want to go.

Since you likely have many people that you *could* contact, and exceptionally little time to do it, you have to **prioritize your outreach**. This is another reason why having a specific goal or target job is really important. For instance, if you already know there is a particular tech company in Silicon Valley that you're interested in working for, then you should start with trying to arrange calls and meetings with anyone you know there (or someone who knows someone there). The same strategy is true for connecting with people in your network who work somewhere with an open position that you're interested in. It is absolutely critical for you to connect with those who are able to help get your resume to the right people in the right places at the right time.

How to connect: *There is simply not a "one size fits all" strategy to how you approach making connections. It will be different for everyone, and how you go about connecting should feel organic to who you are. While you can have a standard template that you use, each specific email, text, or LinkedIn message that you send must be customized and reflect your genuine interest in connecting. The more specific that you can be about why you are reaching out, the better. I have included some ideas and suggested language that you can use and customize to help you get started sending your own messages in the Additional Resources section at the end of this book.*

As you start to meet and speak with people, and apply to more positions, you will have more people to potentially connect with. It's a bit like following a trail of bread crumbs but at the end of it is a pot of gold. You may find that along the way, your initial thoughts about the ideal job have taken you in a new or different direction. Be open to **following your intuition** and take time to really reflect on what you want to do next. With each conversation you have, it's also imperative that you always follow up to thank **EVERYONE** (yes, all caps *and* bold for that one) for their time and help. As someone who has had a lot of these types of conversations, I can't tell you how much this extra bit of thoughtfulness means to someone who has taken some time out of their day to connect and try to help you out. Finally, remember this is a two-way street. Always make sure that you are also thinking of—and offering—ways that you can help the other person, such as making a mutually beneficial introduction to one of your own connections.

In addition to networking, you need to be prepared to invest the time and effort in applying to a *lot* of jobs. Because of the incredible competition for in-house positions, increasing the number of applications that you submit really does increase your odds of success. In my experience, this can be a fairly painstaking process, especially if you're trying to fit it in late at night, early in the morning, or in between family activities over the weekend. Being in the middle of a big trial or trying to close an important deal would also obviously not be the greatest time to begin your in-house search—as much as you might feel like it in those super stressful moments!

A note on timelines: *This whole process will almost always take longer than you think or want it to. For a busy law firm associate, I would anticipate* ***at least six to nine months*** *to allow for the outreach, interviewing, and other components that are necessary for finding your job outside of the firm. Given the pace of hiring at most companies (slow), and demand for in-house jobs (extremely high), it's very rare for anyone to find something in less than three months. There's always exceptions, of course, especially if you happen to work in a really hot area like data privacy. For your sake, I hope that the search goes quickly! Know that if you are already thinking it might be time to start looking for another role, then it probably is. Don't make the mistake of waiting until things are absolutely unbearable at your current job because then you might make a decision that's very reactionary and not aligned with your long-term career goals. Leaving a firm is a serious decision, and you should be sure that you are making it with proper deliberation. By the way—if you already have an in-house job and are looking to make a change to a different company, that takes time as well (about four months in my case). Don't get discouraged and give up your search, even if it takes longer than you might have hoped or expected. The right job for you is out there!*

When you finally do land an interview (and you will) make sure to be fully prepared. Take time to review the interviewing section from Part III, as much of the same guidance is equally applicable when interviewing for in-house roles. Remember, all you can control is your research and preparation, along with your enthusiasm and conviction when you show up for the interview. Do everything that's within your power to knock it out of the park! After you have found that new job (congratulations!), be sure to write back to **everyone** that helped you along the way. Just a short email of thanks and letting them know where you landed is all that you need to do. It doesn't need to be fancy but you do need to send something. Those in your network will greatly appreciate and remember the gesture, trust me.

A WORD ON SECONDMENTS

The term "secondment" essentially means a job rotation where a lawyer is loaned from a law firm to work in-house at a client for a limited period of time—typically three to six months, but it could be shorter or longer. Secondments occur when a client of a firm has a short-term staffing need, which can happen for a variety of reasons. Sometimes it's a backfill for an in-house lawyer who is out on leave, or sometimes it's to help with an unexpected project or surge in work. Regardless of the situation, I think secondments are a fantastic opportunity to gain valuable in-house experience, while still being employed by your firm.

I was able to do a secondment for Sony Pictures which changed the course of my career (and not just because my spouse worked in the office literally next to mine). It gave me highly relevant in-house experience that confirmed my interest in leaving law firm life, and also opened the door (years later) for moving to my current role. Since in-house roles tend to have better work–life balance (although certainly not always), secondments also offer an excellent opportunity to ramp up your in-house job search while you aren't having to bill hours for the firm.

Fun fact! *For anyone curious, the term "secondment" seems to have come from a British military practice of temporarily transferring troops between regiments or corps.*

How do you find a secondment? Again, it can take a bit of luck, but it typically starts with having a very candid conversation with a trusted partner at the firm about your career path and interests. Given that many associates don't make partner at large law firms, helping non-partner track lawyers land a secondment—and potentially a full-time role post-secondment—at a client or potential client can truly be a win-win situation for all involved.

THE BOTTOM LINE: Leaving law firm life and going in-house is a big transition and a wonderful opportunity to do something different in your career journey. It might sound silly, but the most important place to start is actually knowing what your dream job looks like. You need to be able to answer this question: "Can you describe exactly what you are looking for in your next job, and how it fits in with your career goals?" When you have conviction and genuine passion about what you're looking for, others will naturally be drawn to helping you on your journey. If not, it will be difficult to both focus your in-house job search and to articulate to others how they can best help you. You will necessarily need to rely on your professional network to learn of in-house opportunities, get your resume flagged for review by internal recruiters, and maybe even put in a good word for you with the hiring manager.

I found the most frustrating part of trying to find an in-house role was how incredibly arbitrary the whole process could feel at times. It simply isn't possible to predict which specific thing you do, or which specific person that you talk to, will result in eventually getting a job offer. You just have to trust your instincts and focus your time and energy on what you can control. This means you should proactively and genuinely engage with as many people in your network as you can—and apply to as many relevant jobs—within your time and resource constraints. In the inspiring words of Cassandra Sanford: "If this is something that you really want to do, if you believe in it [...] simply keep forging forward because success will come."[40]

IN-HOUSE VISUALIZATION EXERCISE

Visit the Surthriving Law website to download a free copy of this worksheet.

STEP 1: VISUALIZE YOUR IDEAL ROLE

Dream big! Don't limit yourself by what you think is realistic.

Where is it located? ______________________________

What industry? ______________________________

Size of company? ______________________________

Any specific companies of interest? ______________________________

____

Describe what you would be doing there (and if that definitely involves the practice of law): ______________________________

____

____

STEP 2: FOCUSED JOB SEARCH

Spend no more than sixty minutes doing a targeted search on LinkedIn based on parameters identified in Step 1.

List the three most interesting jobs that you found below:

1. ______________________________
2. ______________________________
3. ______________________________

STEP 3: FIRST CONTACT

Who is the one person you already know who is doing something most similar to what you would ideally like to do? This could be someone who works at one of the companies with an open role, or anyone else in your network. Write their name here and—**this is important**—exactly when and how you will contact them (e.g., "Kim Jones. I will email her after I finish work at 6 p.m. tonight.").

Name: ____

Contact plan: ____________________________________

____

____

STEP 4: REFRESH YOUR RESUME

Start by saving a new version of your resume, renamed with your ideal job (something like "In-house Tech Resume – June 2021"). Then go through each of your prior work experiences and add new bullet points for any relevant items that are not on your current resume. It's okay if these are smaller projects, pro bono work, etcetera. Anything that shows your true interests and passion can be relevant to your future job.

STEP 5: MAP YOUR NETWORK & NEXT STEPS

You'll likely need to contact at least ten more people (minimum) before landing your desired position (and possibly many more). Maybe you already have a good idea of a few people to connect with. Maybe someone can introduce you to a few more. Maybe you can reach out to former colleagues or make new connections on LinkedIn. Do you have any "super-connectors" who thrive on making connections? Be sure to pay attention if anyone seems particularly interested in helping you along your path. You can use the below chart to track your progress. Remember: each person will help you get one step closer to the job that you visualized. Always keep that in mind and stay positive along the way!

NAME OF CONTACT & ROLE	METHOD OF CONNECTING	DATE OF MESSAGE

Part V

PARTNER PERSPECTIVES (BIGLAW)

I have never had the distinction of being a law firm partner, nor the motivation to start a firm of my own. But for many law students and practicing lawyers, partnership is the pinnacle of the legal profession. For that reason, I felt compelled to add the perspectives of several amazing lawyers (and just plain great people) in the sections that follow. I hope you find their guest contributions and insights as valuable as I do.

Chapter 18

CURRENT BIGLAW PARTNER

GUEST CONTRIBUTOR: **ALISON MAXWELL**

Is it possible to be a successful partner at a large law firm and still have time to do the things that matter most to you? In this section, one current partner describes how she manages to make it all work—from coaching youth baseball to mentoring young professionals—by prioritizing, being patient (think marathon, not sprint), and having conviction.

My name is Alison Maxwell, and I'm the Deputy Managing Partner for the Seattle office of a global law firm. I also co-chair our firm's national women's affinity group, am the chair of a sub-practice group, and hold various national and international firm committee leadership positions. Outside of work, I coach a traveling youth baseball team and both of my sons' Little League baseball teams. Adam asked me to share my thoughts on (i) the importance of selecting your area of expertise, (ii) how I balance my various activities without letting any (or too many!) balls drop, and finally, (iii) my recommendations for young female professionals.

First things first though, let me give you a little bit of context about myself.

BACKGROUND

I grew up in Ohio and went to college and law school in the Midwest. In college, I studied International Business / Economics and continued my lifelong love of sports as captain of the softball team. I always wanted to be a lawyer so immediately after college, I attended the Ohio State University Moritz College of Law. I always wanted to be a Buckeye and Ohio State was the only law school I applied to.

After law school, my boyfriend (now husband) and I decided we wanted a change from Ohio so we moved to San Francisco. Neither of us had jobs, but we wanted to live there and figured why not. I studied and took the California bar. While doing that, I talked with as many Ohio State alumni in the area that I could so I could learn more about their day-to-day lawyer lives. I knew I wanted to do something transactional and international, but I didn't know what and so those conversations were invaluable. After talking with some international tax lawyers and learning about their practices, I was convinced that international tax was the thing for me.

I then joined Deloitte's international tax group. For non-tax lawyers, this may appear as a somewhat less traditional decision, but it is very common for tax lawyers to work at Big Four accounting firms.

After two years, I had the opportunity to join my current firm's international tax practice in the Bay Area. I jumped at the chance! Why? Because not very many firms have the global platform needed to really provide comprehensive international tax advice, and my firm does.

IMPORTANCE OF SELECTING YOUR AREA OF PRACTICE

I've found that the type of law you practice, as well as the size of firm, can result in *great* variance in your professional experience. I highly recommend that law students talk with as many practicing attorneys as they possibly can so that they can really understand what their day-to-day lives would be like if they work in a particular practice area and for a particular firm or organization.

For example, the life of a tax attorney can be materially different even at the same law firm. I focus on international tax which means that I help corporations understand, manage, and minimize if possible the taxes they pay around the world. I also help corporations as they expand internationally. And, although not 100% tax, a huge part of my practice is helping with large international corporate reorganizations. What this all means is that typically the clients I work with are *my* clients—I get to build long-term relationships with them and I truly aim to become their global trusted advisor. Although I work long hours, for the most part, I have some control over my schedule—granted, I still have calls at 5 a.m. with Europe and 11 p.m. with Asia, but I feel like I have some control. Compare this to M&A [Mergers & Acquisitions] tax attorneys. M&A tax attorneys jump in on many different deals at any given time and more often need to work whenever the deal demands it. And more often, they are less likely to build long-lasting relationship with clients. So the point is, there is a huge difference in an international tax and M&A tax attorney at a large law firm—and these are both tax attorneys. This means the difference between various specialty areas and different employers is enormous. So do your research, talk to as many people as you can, and really think through your preferred area of practice (and firm/organization).

BALANCING IT ALL

Shifting to the topic of work–life balance, you probably noted that I keep quite active both at the firm and outside of firm life. So I'm here to let you know that you *can* still do things that are important to you outside of work at a firm.

There are two absolute key points from my perspective. First, choose a good partner. The only reason I can (try to) balance so many things is that I married an amazing man and we are a team. We tackle everything together.

Second, always be your authentic self. Figure out what you are passionate about and then prioritize those things. For me, I'm passionate about several things. Being a good mom is #1. Also important is being a good role model at work and helping others be their authentic selves, meaning it matters to me that I show others at the firm (both men and women) that you can work and be successful at a big law firm while also being true to yourself. I'm also passionate about coaching.

Is it hard to juggle work, kids, coaching, etcetera? Yes, it is. Does it mean that I get up very, very early to start my day? Yes. But is it absolutely worth it because I have prioritized what is important to me and am doing what I love? Yes.

Once you know that something is important, there are plenty of tactical things that you can do to help stay on track. Some of the things that have helped me most—whether personally or professionally—are:

- **Choosing a good partner.** See above.
- **Finding a good "boss."** I have been very fortunate that I work with an incredible practice group. Our leadership

has always encouraged me to be my authentic self and has always supported me. They have given me leadership and professional opportunities before I even thought I was ready. I have been encouraged to go coach my kids because this time will pass quickly and I will always treasure it. Honestly, I couldn't ask for a better leadership team.

- **Building a good team.** Surround yourself with a group of individuals that puts the team first. Lead by example and have each other's backs. If your co-worker wants to go spend the afternoon with his kids, then step in and help make that happen for him.
- **Finding an outlet for stress.** Figure out what helps you to balance it all and stay sane. For me, that is exercise. I have to exercise. It is the way that I release stress. So figure out what works for you—maybe it is meditation, cooking, gardening, etcetera—and then make time for it.
- **Remembering this is a marathon.** Your legal career is not a sprint. Be patient with yourself. There will be many hard days where you doubt yourself, and feel like you are failing at everything. But sincerely, above all else, believe in yourself.

ADVICE FOR YOUNG FEMALE PROFESSIONALS

Finally, I would be remiss to not highlight the unique challenges that may not be as readily apparent to anyone out there with a profile similar to Adam's (i.e., cisgender, white, male). Often in professional meetings—and certainly on the baseball field—I am the only woman. Sometimes it is hard. Sometimes it is uncomfortable. Sometimes it makes me mad. But most importantly, I try to see it as an amazing opportunity to make a difference—to help other women reach their goals and be their authentic selves.

My advice to other women out there is similar to what I said above—figure out who you are and be true to that. And, believe in yourself. Although I don't like to generalize, unfortunately, in my experience, women tend to doubt themselves more than men.

THE BOTTOM LINE: Each of us only gets to pass this way once. Do it right. Be true to yourself and your passions. And above all else, believe in yourself. If you do these things, then success, as you define it, is pretty much guaranteed.

Chapter 19

FORMER BIGLAW PARTNER

GUEST CONTRIBUTOR: **DANIEL FLOYD SHARES INSIGHT FROM OVER THIRTY YEARS IN BIGLAW**

For many (but by no means all) current and aspiring lawyers, making partner at a law firm is viewed as the end goal of the legal profession. To help pull back the curtain on partnership, this guest contribution offers a candid reflection from a former BigLaw partner on a legal career of more than thirty years at one of the nation's largest and most prestigious firms.

I was a litigation partner at a Vault Law Top 10 law firm for twenty-one years (and spent thirty years in total at the firm), and then made the decision to head up an in-house litigation group at a large entertainment company. While I'm very happy that I made the change, I look back fondly on my career as a BigLaw partner, and feel very fortunate that I chose that career and firm. It was stressful, extremely challenging (intellectually and emotionally), exhausting, financially rewarding, and ultimately perfect for me. Unless you personally know a partner (or better yet, several), it is hard to know what you're really signing up for. I decided to contribute to this surthrival guide because I spent a lot of time on recruiting, training, and mentoring at my firm, and know how hard it is to get meaningful advice.

People want to make partner at law firms for a variety of reasons—opportunity, challenge, prestige, money (not necessarily in that order). I went to public school, then public universities for undergrad and law school. I had no role models or mentors until I clerked for a federal district court judge, so I looked for the best and most prestigious firms, and chose the one that seemed willing to tolerate someone without a lot of polish and who was a first-generation college graduate and lawyer—a firm that would train me and help me become a great lawyer.

I first started thinking and hearing about "partnership track" about five years in. I actually started as a corporate lawyer because I did not think I could handle the public-speaking aspects of being a successful litigator. After a couple of months I realized I was born to be a litigator, so I just worked extremely hard and practiced the performance aspects of the job. Eventually, I felt pretty comfortable in all sorts of stressful situations, although sometimes I'd look down while I was up speaking and my hand would be shaking (and I'd laugh to myself). What really drew me to litigation was legal and factual strategy to address truly complex problems, working with experts, and the one-to-one interaction with witnesses.

Having a mentor at the firm was not critical to my legal career, but working with *many* people, particularly those with different styles, and constantly being open to learning and growing, was absolutely essential. A difficult (but crucial) part of becoming an effective lawyer is learning to operate outside your comfort zone, as your sole purpose should be to represent your clients to the best of your ability.

Here are some specific things about the whole experience of being a partner in a large law firm that don't get widely discussed, or that you might not be aware of early in your career.

1. **Unless you walk in with a lifetime big client, be prepared to work very hard, both as a lawyer and a business developer.** Law firms are constantly competing for business, and successful partners contribute to attracting clients and new matters. Teams are important to win business. As a partner, you're an owner of the firm. There are committee meetings, training, partner meetings and retreats, recruiting events, and business development. And this is all on

top of keeping up on your active matters and constantly looking for new opportunities.

2. **There's a lot of competition.** With rapidly increasing billing rates and other costs, there is a lot of competition—from other big firms, some mid-size firms, and boutiques. While becoming a great lawyer is critical, business development (perhaps unfortunately) has been, and will forever remain, a crucial part of your success. So build relationships and stay in touch, even if you are more of an introvert (like me).

3. **What about billable hours?** There are still definite expectations about billable hours for partners, particularly before you have developed a large client base. Your performance is based on your hours, work you provide for other partners, and most importantly, your ability to provide work for associates, which all leads to revenue. "Leverage" is a concept you will become familiar with.

4. **What's the upside to all this?** Money and professional challenge. At the very top firms, non-equity partners may make $750k to $1.2 million [a year], and for equity partners the pay starts at above [the range of] non-equity partners, and can exceed eight figures for the highest paid. A normal range for equity partners is $1.5 to $3 million for junior partners, and goes all the way up from $7 million to $10 million or more for the

most senior or successful partners. As with everything the amounts vary, but it's indisputable that being a partner at a large law firm is lucrative.

So what made it all worth it for me? The money gave me security and a chance to live well and be charitable and give back for the opportunities I had. What I personally found most rewarding about my years of being a partner was challenging myself to develop and execute legal strategies to address complex and challenging legal problems in a wide range of disciplines (antitrust, securities, legal malpractice, contracts), writing persuasive arguments, and protecting and guiding individuals and companies through challenging times. I also value the many friendships I made, and the clients I represented.

On the flip side, to paraphrase Jerry Maguire, it was a relentless "up-at-dawn, pride-swallowing siege" that no one who hasn't done it will fully understand. No functioning human being can do it just for the money. You have to enjoy the incredible challenge of developing and implementing complex legal strategies, putting yourself on the line to fail, and assuming the burden of the most challenging and financially risky problems of corporations and individuals. And knowing that when you are done, whether or not you are successful, you and your work will forever be associated with a bad memory.

For anyone out there who is just starting out on a legal career of their own and thinking about making partner in

BigLaw one day, here's a few additional pieces of advice. You should focus first on the clients, and represent them to the best of your ability. It is a fiduciary role, and you should never forget that. Good things will follow from that. Your value as a person and lawyer should not be based on whether you become a partner. There are so many factors that you cannot control in a big firm. Challenging yourself, forcing yourself to learn all aspects of being a great lawyer, and never forgetting your fiduciary role will lead to success, however that will be. Remember the economics of firms is based in part on leverage—many more associates than partners. The [size of] incoming classes each year are much larger than the number of partnership promotions for a typical year. Firms are focusing on badly needed expansion of diversity on every level, which provides both opportunities and challenges. Focusing on becoming a great lawyer, with great skill, creativity, integrity, and commitment to your clients will lead to success, I can assure you. No matter how many lawyers are practicing, there is a shortage of great ones.

After thirty years at one firm, five years ago, an opportunity presented itself out of nowhere for me to become head of litigation in-house at an entertainment company. I found it surprisingly easy to jump at the opportunity, even though I had spent almost thirty years, at an average of 2200 billable hours per year—my high was over 2800 (twice) at the firm, with non-chargeable work (committees, business development, pro bono) of several hundreds on top of that.

The main factors in that decision for me were that I was in a personal and financial position where a much better work–life balance was extremely attractive; I liked the idea of having a single client and bringing to bear my life of experience to make sure that client was well-represented in the world of litigation; and I liked the idea of working with a small team day to day. The move has exceeded my expectations. I have moments where I miss the intensity and challenges of my prior life, but I derive great happiness and satisfaction from solving problems, big and small, for an organization that I admire.

So what does life look like working in-house in 2021 and beyond for me? I've found my home for the rest of my career, unless something unforeseen takes the decision out of my hands. In that case, I'll find something, maybe even going back to a firm. I had thought I might want to be a judge, but that ship has passed.

In terms of final thoughts reflecting on this entire experience, I think the most important thing I wished that I had known when I started was that being extremely devoted to representing my clients would (generally) lead to good results for them, personal satisfaction for me, and financial security for my family. The stress was often exhausting, and often self-imposed.

THE BOTTOM LINE: Throwing yourself in headfirst and working hard at the *right* law firm can help make your career, whether you choose to stay or not. It will provide you opportunities you cannot get on your own, and provide you with options—you can stay and work to make partner, you can go in-house, to government, or another firm—while being well paid. It will never be easy. But if you focus on the work, the clients, and your obligations as a lawyer, it can be personally and professionally satisfying.

Part VI

BEYOND BIGLAW

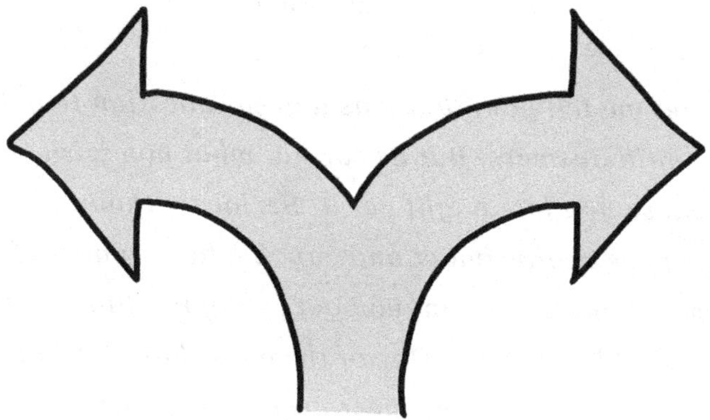

As mentioned earlier in this guide, I took time to solicit and collect feedback from a number of current law students prior to publication. One question that I asked was the following:

Putting on your most critical *New York Times* book reviewer hat (or that of a snarky internet reviewer troll), what's the WORST thing you might write in your review based on what you've seen so far? (e.g., "Part I seems to be a glorified series of product reviews that probably could have been done as a blog post versus an actual book. Hard to see the value here." Or maybe, "The author seems totally out of touch with the needs of current law students.")

Let me tell you, that was a great question to get candid answers. But be careful what you wish for, because you just might get it! Seriously though, when you ask really smart and capable law students for their honest opinion, you get really intelligent and actionable answers. One of the ones that stood out to me said simply: "The most useful books for students provide numerous perspectives. Try including others." Other feedback in a similar vein included:

- *"Be wary of speaking only from the perspective of BigLaw and in-house."*

- *"Author seems to assume BigLaw is a universal or desired experience and neglects the wide diversity of students and their prospective paths."*

- *"This book might seem bad to public interested/ nonprofit/social justice interested law students."*

I heard this feedback loud and clear. I took some of my own advice and tried networking to connect with others who could offer additional perspectives for you to consider. Without further ado, here is their insight and advice on important areas beyond BigLaw.

Chapter 20

CO-FOUNDING A FIRM

GUEST CONTRIBUTOR: **HEIDI BRADLEY, CO-FOUNDER OF BRADLEY BERNSTEIN SANDS LLP (BBS)**

After fifteen years in BigLaw, this guest contributor co-founded her firm in 2020. In this contribution she explains how it has been one of the most challenging and rewarding experiences she's had in her entire career.

My name is Heidi Bradley, and Adam asked me to share my perspective about launching my own small law firm after working in BigLaw for fifteen years. Launching your own firm isn't for everyone. To be honest, I never even really thought it was for me! But there were a number of things that made me feel like it was not only possible, but also a really good move for me at this point in my career. So I thought it might be helpful to share a bit about what pushed me in the direction of founding my own firm, and some practical advice if you think it might be something you'd like to consider at some point in your career.

First, a little bit about my background, and how I ended up founding my firm. I graduated from Stanford Law School in 2004, and went to work at Heller Ehrman LLP, which was a top law firm headquartered in San Francisco. I had a good run at Heller until the economic meltdown of 2008, when the 120-year-old firm went under overnight. It was shocking, to say the least. I was extremely fortunate to be able to land another associate position right away at Sullivan & Cromwell (S&C) in Los Angeles. I chose S&C because after seeing my former firm go under, I wanted to be at a place that would definitely stay in business through the economic downturn! I never intended to stay permanently at S&C, but I did stay for seven years before I made a move back to my hometown of Seattle. In Seattle, I joined a regional law firm, Lane Powell, as a partner. I also had a good run at Lane Powell, becoming a co-leader of the litigation department and developing some strong client relationships of my own, [which was] something that was more challenging at S&C, where so many clients are huge, institutional clients.

So why leave the steady gig as head of litigation at a well-respected regional law firm to do my own thing? For me, the decision was driven largely by a desire for more self-determination in shaping the direction and values of my firm. It was also a financial decision. As an equity partner, I had more visibility into how many of the dollars I brought in went to overhead rather than into my pocket or the pockets of the wonderful associates and others I worked with. Don't get me wrong—the firm was very well run and I had a good deal of confidence in its leadership and overall direction. But once I started to think about launching my own firm, I was particularly intrigued by the idea of building something from the ground up, with partners I chose, and with a financial future in which I had more control.

Still, like many lawyers, I am generally risk-averse, and the thought of launching my own firm was pretty terrifying. I certainly had some days where I wondered if leaving my stable equity partner position in the middle of a pandemic was the right decision. Spoiler alert: for me, launching BBS has been a great move, and I've become a big fan of thinking beyond BigLaw as you consider your career path.

One of the big obstacles to launching a new firm can be the logistics of it all—the business licenses, insurance, building a website, opening bank accounts, finding and furnishing office space, setting up computers and servers, and hiring staff. It's a *lot* to navigate. We actively planned our launch for about six months before going live. And most of those logistical hurdles also cost money. Some new firms secure small business loans to help fund their start-up expenses, but my partners and I chose to keep our start-up expenses as low as possible, and to self-fund the expenses from our personal savings.

For us, keeping our start-up expenses low meant holding off on getting office space (which was easier in the pandemic), and also launching without hiring any staff or associates. Going without staff or associates after working in large law firms for my whole career was one of the biggest adjustments in terms of my day-to-day work. I've learned a lot about formatting my own briefs, creating tables of authorities, electronic filing, and printing labels for service by mail. Not to mention drafting discovery and briefs all on my own (something I hadn't had to do since I was an associate myself). And while I'm excited that we're now at a point in the firm where we're ready to hire some help, it has been surprisingly empowering to learn how to do all these things myself.

Another thing that might feel like a big obstacle to launching your own firm is the perception that the only people who can be successful in their own firms are lawyers who already have big books of their own business. That's not necessarily the case. Of course, launching a firm with lots of ongoing work from clients who you can definitely count on to move their business with you is the best-case scenario, but there are lots of ways to build your business. In my experience, it mostly comes back to the same things that will make you successful as a lawyer in any setting: doing a great job for the clients you do have, and building a strong referral network of lawyers who will think of you when they need a lawyer with your particular specialty. For a small firm, I've found that it's also particularly important to have a strong online presence that will help give prospective clients a sense of your background and credibility.

When we launched BBS, we had a handful of clients with ongoing cases, but not enough to keep us busy full-time. We devoted those early weeks to building even stronger relationships with our existing clients, while also spending a lot of time networking, marketing, and working through the many logistics of having a brand-new firm. But even with less than a full plate of billable work right out of the gate, we felt confident that we could make ends meet financially. Just to give a rough sketch of the math—billing just 100 hours a month at $500 per hour (for example) adds up to a pretty respectable living, even after accounting for overhead.

That's not to say that the financial path has been easy from the beginning. Even with a good amount of work on day one, we went three or four months where we didn't pay ourselves anything. That's because it takes a really long time from the day we do the work until the day we finally get paid for the work, even with clients who pay promptly (and they don't all pay promptly!). Life feels a lot better now that we have cash coming in monthly, but there were some lean months, particularly after self-funding our start-up costs.

Nine months after [launching] our new firm, life feels a lot better in other ways too. My desire to found a firm that reflected my values and my strategic vision has become a reality in more ways than I ever expected. My partners and I have been able to launch initiatives that would have taken years to develop at a larger firm (e.g., the BBS Fellowship program),[41] and we've created a firm culture that emphasizes things we care about. We've been able to take on big, important pro bono projects, and we've developed even stronger relationships with clients old and new.

Not every day is super fun—like I mentioned, I draft my own discovery responses now! And I do sometimes miss the collegiality of working on big teams with associates, paralegals, legal assistants, and other partners. I also spend a lot more time on firm administrative tasks than I did when I was a partner in a bigger firm. But that part is much more tolerable (even enjoyable) when I'm doing it to build my own firm. It can also be stressful in ways that are different from the stress of working in BigLaw. The general ebbs and flows of litigation hit us harder at our small firm. When it's really busy, there are no extra bodies to throw at a big project. And when things slow down, we see it in our firm bank account. But even with all of that, not a day goes by when I regret the decision to launch my own firm. It took guts, but I'm proud of what we've built, and I can't wait to see what the future holds for BBS.

THE BOTTOM LINE: Launching your own small firm is not for the faint of heart. It takes lots of logistical planning, start-up capital, serious business development, and a willingness to take on a lot more risk than many lawyers are comfortable with. But if you're willing to take the leap, you may be able to build exactly the type of law firm you've always wished you could work for.

Chapter 21
CLERKSHIPS

GUEST CONTRIBUTOR: **CURRENT FEDERAL CLERK (ANONYMOUS)**

Many current law students and practicing lawyers are interested in potentially clerking at some point in their legal careers. The following section provides a candid "behind the scenes" look from the vantage point of a current federal clerk on what the experience has been like thus far in their clerkship.

I had been clerking for a federal district court judge for about six months when Adam messaged me on LinkedIn about this project. After a brief chat, he asked if I would be willing to answer the question: "What do I wish I had known before I applied for the clerkship?" These are my candid thoughts on the answer to that question based on my experience. As you'll see below, a lot can depend on the judge who you ultimately clerk for, as there can be quite a bit of variance. But I can say (and I think this goes for most clerks) that it's a tremendous opportunity. I'm already a better lawyer, I've made some great relationships (professionally and personally), and I got a bit of a break from BigLaw! More on that to come...

To start, what is a clerkship? As a judicial law clerk, you are essentially a judge's full-time research and writing assistant. Clerks research and draft opinions and orders, and depending on the judge, may also be asked to manage case dockets (e.g., address routine filings and prepare for status hearings). You can apply for a clerkship at the federal level or the state level and in an appellate court or a trial/district court; there are also clerkships available with magistrate judges, in the bankruptcy courts, and other specialized courts. Bottom line—there are lots of opportunities if you're thinking about clerking.

And if you are thinking about it, let's dispel the myth of *getting a clerkship is out of my league* right now. I went to a pretty competitive law school, where top students in the class were mostly handpicked by professors and got a lot of help navigating the clerkship application process. I was not one of those top students (thanks a lot, property and contracts exams), and I never got that tap on the shoulder. I made up my mind that clerking was not in the cards for me and proceeded with my BigLaw plans.

Fast forward a few years—I was wrong! At the three-year mark at the law firm ("the three-year BigLaw itch"), I got a call out of the blue from an old law school classmate. He said a judge in my judicial district was looking to fill a clerkship spot immediately. I jumped on it. I got my application in within a few days, and... I didn't get it. But that lit a fire, and after one more rejection, I was offered a clerkship position with a really great judge.

To break down the timing and application process a bit further, I applied as an "alumni clerk" (i.e., a few years out of law school). You can also apply during law school to start the clerkship following graduation. Through your research about different judges, you'll find that some judges prefer hiring recent law school grads, and some judges prefer hiring clerks with a few years of work experience. Most federal judges accept applications through a formal centralized database, the Online System for Clerkship Application and Review (OSCAR). Some federal judges accept applications through informal processes (e.g., sending applications via email or hard copies to a judge's chambers). The state court clerkship application processes vary state by state. Whatever the process, your application package typically includes a cover letter, resume, transcript, writing sample, and two, often three, letters of recommendation.

A few tips on the application package: First, be sure to highlight any relevant research and writing experience in your cover letter and resume (that's the job after all!). Second, it's always good to research the judge and include a line (or two) in your cover letter about why you want to work for that judge specifically (e.g., you admire his/her path to the bench, you've connected with a former clerk and heard about what a great mentor the judge is, etcetera). Third, proofread, and I mean *really* proofread. One misspelling could be a make it or break it for this job.

After you've sent in your application, the next step in the process is the interview. You will often interview with the current law clerks first and then the judge (could be one or two interviews with the judge). My judge asked mostly behavioral questions as part of my two interviews (e.g., tell me about your work experience, what are some of your strengths, and why do you want to clerk). But some judges ask more substantive questions, expecting applicants to have read a large sample of issued opinions and have a sense of their ruling record. This is where talking to former law clerks and working with your school's clerkship coordinator comes in handy. They will be able to give you a good idea of what to expect in your interviews.

Pro tip: *Even if you are out of law school and applying as an alumnus, call your alma mater's clerkship coordinator. I assure you they will be ready and willing to help (the schools want as many students as possible, current or former, to clerk; it's good for their stats).*

Bonus pro tip: *The most important advice I can give about clerkship interviews (as cliché as it sounds) is be yourself. The chambers staff is very small; judges want to find someone they can work with closely for at least a year and sometimes two years (again, depends on the judge). The interview is more about fit than anything else.*

Once you've secured the position (congratulations!), you have to let your boss know that you're leaving (if you're working). This wasn't too bad for me, as I was fairly open with my law firm partners that I was interested in applying for a clerkship position at some point. Whatever you're doing before your clerkship, I would definitely recommend giving yourself a minimum of two weeks off for transition time between jobs. I took, if you can believe it, one day off (I had to extend my email access through Sunday night at midnight to wrap up some projects). Don't do that! Give yourself a chance to recharge before your start date.

And then you're clerking! What should you expect? It shouldn't be a surprise by now—a *lot* of research and writing. You'll have Westlaw (for case research) on one computer screen and Microsoft Word on the other for about ten hours a day. You'll read the parties' briefs, parse through the legal issues, draft the opinion, edit the opinion, and then the judge will issue your opinion. You'll find yourself going to your co-clerks and the judge with questions throughout the typically two to three-week drafting process, and you're often wrestling with some tough issues. Once the opinion is issued, you pick up your next. In a year, I expect to write about fifty opinions.

My pandemic clerkship experience has been unique in the sense that I was in chambers (safely masked and socially distant from others) for the first two months, and now I am working from home most days. While we're not observing as many hearings, technology (namely, Track Changes) has made the opinion writing process fairly easy from home.

Oh, and you are probably wondering about the whole salary part of the equation. Short answer: it really varies. A salary for a law clerk employed by a federal district court judge is determined by a special government pay scale (based on your number of years of work experience) plus local cost of living. To put it in approximate numbers, anywhere from $50k to $100k.

And my hours? They aren't bad, and *definitely* better than the firm. So yes, it's true you can have a bit more of a life when clerking!

And what's next for me after clerking? Great question. The answer is I'm not exactly sure. One option is to continue clerking for another year. Other common options are going back to a law firm or applying for government or in-house positions. At the end of the day, it will ultimately depend on the bigger picture and spending some time reflecting myself on some of the questions in other parts of this surthrival guide!

So, we've been over the *how* and the *what* to expect, but we've saved perhaps the most important question for last—the *why*. Why clerk? It's often a pay cut if you're coming from a law firm job. It's very academic and sometimes a bit solitary—no running from meeting to meeting, courtroom to courtroom. So why do it? I think the most common reason (and maybe not the best reason) is that clerking is very "prestigious." Your law school and other lawyers will tell you that if you clerk, most doors are open for you. And in a lot of cases, that's true. It is prestigious! But I think to get the most out of the experience that can't be the only reason you apply. As nerdy as it sounds, you also have to like learning and like THE LAW. Because that's what you'll be doing day in and day out. A good point of reference (and the turn-off for many of my transactional lawyer friends) is if you don't like law school, you might not like clerking.

THE BOTTOM LINE: My reasons for applying for clerkship were a mix of the "good" and the "bad." I knew it was prestigious, and I hoped it would get me to the next thing, whatever that is. But I also was excited for the challenge, interested in sharpening some of those lawyer skills, and frankly, wanted a break from the law firm hours. I'm really happy I did apply. In fact, I wish I'd had the confidence to apply earlier than I did. If you're interested, go for it.

Chapter 22

GOVERNMENT SERVICE

GUEST CONTRIBUTOR: **CURRENT FEDERAL LAWYER (ANONYMOUS)**

Working as a lawyer for the government can vary a great deal depending on whether it's federal or state, criminal or civil, in a large or small town. The following section provides a comprehensive look at what the career path of a current federal prosecutor has been, what the job actually entails, and future opportunities after government service.

I have worked as prosecutor for the federal government for over eight years after a lengthy legal career working at large law firms. If you don't already know someone who works as a lawyer for the government then it can be pretty difficult to know what to expect. I agreed to share my candid thoughts and perspective so you can have at least one view from the inside of what it's like.

People choose government service for a variety of reasons.

Many lawyers, at least at the federal level, are fleeing life at large law firms, or opting to forgo private practice salaries in the pursuit of "on your feet" courtroom experiences. And while that certainly factored into my decision, I was primarily motivated by the client: justice. As corny as that sounds (and as corny as it is), after a decade in private practice of representing the interests of businesses and individuals regardless of whether my moral compass aligned with that of my clients, I wanted a job that enabled me to ask just one simple question when making all decisions: "Is this the 'right' thing to do?" Of course, one can debate what "right" means in certain situations. But there is something freeing about practicing law where that is your only guiding principle. It's not about "winning." It's not about "losing." The practice of law, as a prosecutor, is about "doing justice" every day.

The lawyers I see who enjoy this type of practice the most are generally motivated by a commitment to public service.

This is a very difficult job. There can (and should be) lots of pressure on those who choose to do it. After all, the decisions we make have severe consequences on individuals and the larger community. We put people in jail in an effort to keep society safer. That is an awesome responsibility and we have to ensure we are right when making those decisions. People not motivated by a desire to serve the public in this fashion burn out over time. I mean, why stay? The pay is lousy. The resources suck. And, if you do everything right, the best you can hope for is [that] some nameless bureaucrat gives you a certificate printed in black and white that says you did a good job. Those who stay, stay because they are motivated by a greater calling. And the fact that the job itself enables us to make a small difference to the greater community is what we enjoy the most about it.

What I personally have found the most rewarding about being a prosecutor is the autonomy.

The government is often categorized (particularly by defense attorneys) as having unlimited resources. While in many ways that may be true, nothing could be further from the truth with respect to staffing of government lawyers to cases. In most instances, you will be the only lawyer staffed on a case from its inception to its conclusion. Daunting as that may be (at least initially), it results in a happy by-product: near-complete autonomy at every stage of a matter. You are the decision maker on nearly every matter involving your cases. Of course, you have colleagues and supervisors to discuss close calls with or bounce questions off of. But, as a prosecutor, the final decision rests with you. Gone are the days of having to seek approval of seven layers of senior lawyers at your law firm and your client before you can send an email that says: "Are you available for a call next Wednesday?"

How do you get a job working as a lawyer in government?

Like most things, it depends. For competitive jobs, like a federal prosecutor in a major city, the process usually takes time. It requires applicants to have spent several years practicing law elsewhere—be it private practice or in state government—honing their skills as more junior attorneys. Rarely are there opportunities to become a federal prosecutor straight out of law school or a clerkship. Even after getting that experience (roughly five to ten years depending on the position), it often takes several rounds of submitting applications to even get an interview. As for interviews, they can vary from one-on-ones to panels of multiple lawyers at one time. And in most offices, there are several rounds of interviews (I've heard of people being called back five or six times) that culminate with an interview by a political appointee in charge of the office.

Almost no one has the right experience for the job—those coming from private practice lack "on your feet" experience, while those coming from state government lack the large-scale litigation experience—so many applicants have the experience of being interviewed and rejected multiple times before getting an offer. As others have explained to me, and as was my experience, the sine qua non of getting a job as a government attorney is giving up on getting a job as a government attorney. Only then will the offer arrive. The application standards become somewhat less strict outside of major population centers, so your odds may improve if you are willing to move for a job. But there are also fewer positions in more rural communities, so even being willing to move does not guarantee success.

If you get an offer, congratulations are in order, but the job is not yours yet. For most federal positions, there is an extensive background check, drug testing (remember, marijuana is still a no-no at the federal level), and interviews of yourself, your family and friends, and others conducted by federal agents. This process can take a number of months depending on the backlog. Only after you clear the background check can you begin as a government lawyer, so, while most people pass the background check, don't leave your current job until you get word that you passed.

For me, the process took two years from start (my first application) to finish (clearing my background check). For some the process will undoubtedly go quicker, but for many, it will take much longer.

Here are some specific things about the application and interview process that I wish I had known back then when I was first applying:

First, be patient. As discussed earlier, the application process is likely going to take lots of time and effort. It will involve a lot of rejection. Don't get discouraged. If you want the job badly enough, keep at it. Between rejection and your next application, take the opportunity to work on your weaknesses to show progress. For example, if you are coming from private practice, take on matters (whether for paying clients or pro bono) that enable you to gain practical courtroom skills.

Second, network. Whether it should be this way or not, government positions (like most) are easier to get when you know someone in the office (or know someone who has connections to those in the office) who can vouch for you. This can start as early as law school by interning or externing in the office you want to work when you gain enough experience. After law school, target employers who have well-connected alumni from the government position that you wish to join. As a junior attorney, ask to work with those government alumni. Simply put, build a network of advocates who will help advance your application.

Third, be prepared. You have spent the better part of a decade trying to get this job. Don't blow it in the interview. Take a deep breath and try to relax. There is nothing more off-putting in an interview than an applicant who comes across overly intense to the point that you wouldn't want to work with her. After all, while those of us interviewing you are prosecutors and prone to having reputations as being serious, we are also looking for someone who will be a good colleague. But part of being a good colleague is also being prepared—which a surprising number of applicants simply aren't during their interview. Do some homework on the cases your interviewers have handled, know why you want to become a prosecutor, and think about your weaknesses as a candidate and how you think you can compensate for them. And though this should go without saying (but requires it because I've interviewed an applicant wearing a T-shirt), dress appropriately. Think of this as your first court appearance on behalf of the government—don't come underdressed or unprepared.

Once you've been through all that, you have to let your current employer know your plans.

Hopefully you listened to my advice regarding networking, so your current employer will already know that you are interviewing. But even if you were like me and kept it a secret until you got the job offer, most employers are happy to learn that they will have an alum joining the ranks of the federal government. The background check process also takes so long that you should have more than sufficient time to transition your caseload to someone else at your current employer so no one will be left in a precarious position by your departure.

Whatever you're doing before your start date, I recommend giving yourself at least a couple weeks off between jobs if you can afford to do so.

This is classic "do what I say, not what I do" advice. I left my position in private practice on a Friday and started my job in government the following Monday. At the time, my rationale for taking no time off was that I had been in "quasi-unemployment" for months during the background check process at my old firm. So, while I was still working to transition my caseload, I felt as if I had been on holiday (compared to my old routine) for some time. In hindsight, I should have taken time off to give myself a mental break. Although it is true that I had been working less than normal, I still had work responsibilities up until the last minute—heck, on my last day my firm contemplated flying me on a six-hour round trip to retrieve documents (they ultimately sent someone more junior).

There are rarely times in life when we have absolutely no work-related responsibilities hanging over our heads, [times when] we can completely reset, reconnect with ourselves and loved ones, and, at a minimum, just catch up on some long-overdue sleep. Take as much time as possible. I promise you will not regret it.

Let's talk about the day-to-day job—what do I actually do most days?

Most people believe that prosecutors spend the vast majority of their time in court. Trials. Sentencings. Appeals. Arguing to judges and juries. You know, "You can't handle the truth"-like stuff. While we certainly do all of the above, our public-facing work is just the tip of the iceberg. What may be a surprise to many is that most of our job involves building cases together with our law enforcement partners, like the FBI. That is because at the federal level, most of our work is proactive rather than reactive. In other words, we actively build cases instead of simply waiting for them to come to us. We aren't typically prosecuting the guy who gets caught by a patrol car selling drugs on the street corner; we are trying to take down the gang who supplies the drugs and terrorizes that community. And to build these types of cases often takes months, if not years, of painstaking, behind-the-scenes work. Directing undercover agents. Interviewing cooperating (and sometimes not so cooperative) witnesses, subjects, and targets. Using legal process, such as wiretaps, search warrants, or subpoenas, to gather mountains of evidence. Presenting this evidence to grand juries. And finally, making charging recommendations. Only then, after charging, do our investigations make it into the public arena. From there, the job becomes in many (albeit it not all) ways similar to civil practice: motion practice, discovery, plea negotiations, and trial preparation.

In some ways the pandemic has changed my job, and it other ways it remains the same. For starters, the public-facing aspects of my job (i.e., the court appearances) have mostly become virtual. As a result, rather than travel to the office to attend hearings, most days I work remotely since the office's finest (1980s) technology does not work well with virtual court appearances. That said, after some initial glitches, the investigation side of the job has remained, with some minor adaptations (e.g., electronically swearing out warrants), largely unchanged.

Oh, and you probably are wondering about the whole salary part of the equation.

Short answer: it varies widely. Federal positions pay more than state positions, but state positions pay more than local ones. The Securities and Exchange Commission pays more than the Department of Justice (DOJ). But working for the DOJ in Washington, D.C. pays more than working for a competent of the DOJ someplace outside of Washington, D.C. Generally speaking, for a federal prosecutor, the pay range is roughly from $60,000 to $200,000 depending on the role and your seniority level. For any specific job, at the federal level, you should be able to find a posting with details about compensation for the position on the agency's website. However, even lawyers with several years of experience should expect to receive an offer towards the lower end of the salary range indicated in the posting.

What about my hours?

Working for the government allows you to have more control over your schedule, and, accordingly, more of a work–life balance than in private practice. That said, in my experience, the total number of hours I work is not significantly less than my time in private practice. It is certainly true that some people come to government for the nine-to-five schedule, but, as with anything, if you only put in the bare minimum you will miss out on the best cases. So while it is possible to work significantly less than in private practice, you will miss out if you don't put in the effort. Plus, it feels a lot less like "work" when you get to decide when to do something rather than some client or partner imposing the deadline on you.

So what does life look like next?

Great question—the answer is I'm not exactly sure. One option is to keep doing this until I retire. Another common option is going back to a firm but, unless the perfect opportunity presents itself, I think that is unlikely. More and more of my colleagues have been hired by companies seeking the skill set of a prosecutor, such as internal investigation groups at major public companies.

Final thoughts reflecting on my entire experience:

I think the most important thing I wish that I had known back when I was earlier in my career (i.e., before government service) is to focus more on the big picture. Often times, especially as a more junior attorney, I would get so caught up in whatever issue or project was immediately before me. I was obsessed with making the next thing—next brief, next document production, next deposition, next meet-and-confer letter—perfect. In so doing, I lost track. I floated from project to project, without reflecting on how they all fit together for my case. But more importantly, I also lost track of how these projects could help me in my career. Rather than proactively plotting a course from where I was to where I wanted to be, I drifted endlessly from discrete project to discrete project. I had developed what I was told was a good reputation as an associate (mainly because I would give everything my all) but I had done so to my own detriment. Other associates more focused on where they wanted to go in their careers ended up working for the "better" partners, getting on the "better" projects, and generally doing more to advance themselves when they were younger. Now, I'm certainly not advocating that people become motivated solely by self-interest. But I certainly could have benefited by a little more focus on my larger career goals and how my day-to-day choices were helping (or harming) my ability to reach them.

THE BOTTOM LINE: Former prosecutors often tell me that I, as a prosecutor, have the best legal job there is. Not being clairvoyant, I can't say with certainty they are right. But what I can say is that it is the best legal job that I have ever had. And I'd be hard-pressed to think of a more exciting, challenging, and rewarding job. The only downside is the pay (which, even at the federal level, pales in comparison to most first-year associates at big law firms). But if it paid more, you'd probably never have the chance to get the job since none of us would ever leave.

Chapter 23

PUBLIC INTEREST LAW

GUEST CONTRIBUTOR: **MONICA MILLER, LEGAL DIRECTOR AND SENIOR COUNSEL, AMERICAN HUMANIST ASSOCIATION; LEGAL WORKING GROUP LEADER, NONHUMAN RIGHTS PROJECT**

Know anyone who has argued a case before the Supreme Court of the United States, appeared in an HBO documentary, and who holds positions at two different nonprofit organizations? If not, meet Monica Miller and prepare to learn all about the deep passion she brings to her public interest practice.

My name is Monica Miller and I was asked to contribute my perspective for anyone who might not be completely sold on BigLaw and/or is thinking about a possible career change.

I hope that by contributing I can help you determine whether public interest law might be a career path that will have as much meaning and significance for you as it has had for me. I also want to offer some pragmatic tips for those who choose to embark on this challenging but rewarding pathway.

I've known since I was a child that I wanted to work on animal rights in some capacity. In fact, I wanted to be an "animal cop" for the longest time. But a path to that goal wasn't always obvious. The only thing clear to me was that there was no clearly delineated "animal rights" academic track when I entered undergrad (2004). So I went with the closest alternative that I could find: Environmental Studies.

I chose Pitzer College in Southern California for its leading environmental and social justice curriculum. While there, I taught art in prisons, environmental science to fifth graders, and took the first-ever Sociology of Secularism class. In 2009, I graduated from Columbia University with my master's degree in Public Administration for Environmental Science and Policy. I went on to Vermont Law School (VLS), then the top environmental law school and one of only a handful that offered any course on animal law.

During my first year of law school, I attended an animal law conference in Portland, Oregon, where I saw Steven Wise give a talk on animal personhood, i.e., the very cause that drove me to law school. Steve was seeking volunteers to work for his new group, the Center for the Expansion of Nonhuman Rights, which would later become the Nonhuman

Rights Project (NhRP). I took the initiative of following up with him directly and volunteered with his group for my remaining two years of law school (about ten to twenty hours per week). Steve is now my boss at NhRP and our work from [my time in] law school paved the way for historic animal rights litigation that I'm at the forefront of now—so never underestimate how important being proactive can be, especially while in law school.

While at VLS, I also solidified my growing concern for the separation of church and state guaranteed by the First Amendment. I started the Secular Law Student Association and applied for a summer legal internship at the American Humanist Association (AHA) where I would work on Establishment Clause cases. I ended up drafting a Supreme Court amicus brief and a Seventh Circuit amicus brief that summer, with minimal input by the legal director at the time. That experience was so thrilling (for this 1L anyway), I applied to AHA for my Semester in Practice and then stayed on through for a second summer internship. I highly recommend getting any sort of this very practical experience while in school as it can be so helpful later in your career. Moreover, if there is an organization that you know you want to work for, I highly recommend applying for an internship there as early as possible.

The AHA also offered me the first-ever staff attorney position months before my graduation. Like an ambitious maniac, I accepted both positions after convincing my respective bosses it was totally doable. I'm still that maniac. Since graduating in 2012 until present (2021), I still work vigorously for both organizations in a full-time and part-time capacity, my sanity aside (more on that piece below). To this day, I wonder if either boss has ever read my law school resume.

So how do you go about getting that first "foot in the door" at a nonprofit doing work that you care about deeply? That may be tricky and may require quite a bit of persistence. Steve actually did not receive (or ignored) the first email I sent him looking to volunteer. I waited until I was enrolled in my Animal Law class (the only one at the time) and then emailed him to see if there was any topic I could research for my Animal Law paper that would benefit his group. Regarding my AHA internship, as soon as I knew I was interested in separation of church and state law, I contacted a lawyer based in California, Michael Newdow, who had filed several prominent Establishment Clause cases, and asked if he needed research help. He was enthused about the offer for help (he just took his cases pro bono and solo) and I ended up doing several significant research/writing projects for him my first semester of law school. This gave me a great (though unplanned) name-drop boost for my AHA interview, as the legal director was familiar with Newdow's cases. So when in doubt, I would recommend always trying to reach out to someone if you have a genuine interest in supporting the work that they are doing.

I also want to shed some light on how to figure out what types of organizations actually hire public interest lawyers. I think that the best place to start is an internship or externship. What's the application and interview process like at the organizations where I work? We post the position on our website, LinkedIn, and maybe a few other sites. My paralegal and I will comb through the applications and make three categories: Yes/Maybe/No. Where you went to law school is way less important to me than your proven ability to write well and work independently. It's also critical to know the organization's mission *before* your interview and to also be aware of the group's most recent cases.

Practicing public interest law has many benefits, particularly if you are able to find opportunities in newer or growing organizations where you can gain some autonomy early in your career. In contrast to large law firm life—where associates typically get little client visibility and almost no opportunity to serve as lead counsel early in their careers—public interest lawyers are typically thrown into the fire. Being the only lawyer (or one of only two lawyers, depending on the year) at the AHA turned me into a seasoned federal litigator on a fairly expedited track. I've now served as lead counsel in over thirty First Amendment cases, and I've argued in the Fourth (twice), Fifth, Ninth, and Eleventh Circuit Courts and the U.S. Supreme Court. Before she passed, I argued in front of Ruth Bader Ginsburg. I've been quoted in every major media outlet, some several times. I've been live on

MSNBC, Fox, NPR, and other network programs. My work at the NhRP (along with my law school bangs) is featured in an HBO documentary, *Unlocking the Cage*.

On the flip side, a career in public interest law has many unique challenges. With less (or no) support staff, it often means many long hours at lower compensation. My caseload has been chronically extreme—for the bulk of my career, I have juggled ten federal cases at a time. One month I had a Tenth Circuit brief due, a Fifth Circuit oral argument, a discovery deadline, and a speaking event. The first time I took a deposition, I didn't take just one. I took fifteen (school officials at a major Colorado school district) in a small room, and I kept trying to channel my inner *Law and Order*. I never learned how to take a deposition; I just went with the "fake it 'til you make it" attitude. I'm sure I overlooked objections I shouldn't have, and committed some violations of some sort, but by the fifth depo, opposing counsel checked out and it was smooth sailing.

Speaking of that deposition day, many of us are plagued with imposter syndrome. I don't look like a constitutional lawyer. I don't talk like a constitutional lawyer. I've been stopped by security at numerous federal courthouses who have told me to use the "juror door." In the U.S. District Court of Florida (Northern), the security did not believe I was arguing counsel and even confiscated my phone and my water bottle and refused to let me pass. The court clerk went out and admonished them and created quite the scene.

Other challenges faced when working for smaller non-profits include being expected to answer "in-house" (i.e., corporate law) legal questions that are outside of your expertise, which can add extra stress and time to an already demanding workload. Moreover, you may be asked to do projects for which you probably don't require a law degree. Examples of tasks I've regularly been assigned include: writing articles for magazines, tabling at annual conferences, attending donor events and lunches, speaking to local chapters about our work, running the Instagram account, drafting and editing press releases and so on.

What about my hours? I have virtually no free time. Most of my career I've worked in the range of 9 a.m. to 10 p.m. but countless nights were much later. I saw more sunrises from all-nighters prepping for my Supreme Court case than I saw in my four years of college and three years in law school combined. What am I doing all of those hours on most days? Write. Research. Draft a habeas corpus petition on behalf of an elephant. Draft an Eleventh Circuit brief on the Establishment Clause. Send a demand letter to a school district. Talk to a reporter. Lead a staff meeting. Confer with my paralegal. Record a "Legal Tuesdays" video, attend a hearing, moot another lawyer's oral argument.

Finally, I would be remiss not to touch on emotional exhaustion and compassion fatigue. If you are working in a sector that deals with a heavy issue—be it animal abuse, child abuse, racism, environmental degradation, etcetera—

you are immersing yourself in something potentially traumatizing, which can quickly yield mental health problems and/or burnout. Some folks get desensitized. Others get traumatized. Anyone entering a field like this must have a therapist lined up or a support system for harder days. I personally try to avoid as much negative news and graphic images of abuse as I can (without being ignorant on a topic I need to be informed of). I don't need to see another cow suffer to know not to eat meat. Seeing another abusive image will not make me a better advocate, but it could make me a more fatigued one. I also practice daily meditation on the Sam Harris Waking Up app. I use a workout app called Freeletics. These apps make it easy for me to keep my mental health in check.

Physical and mental exhaustion are not the only downsides to the nonprofit lawyer career. It's safe to say that most people who follow a path to public interest aren't doing it just for the money. If you have huge student loans this can make things challenging. The debt forgiveness program could be availing to some folks. Others just make it work.

But perhaps most importantly, I find value in the work I do. At the NhRP, I am litigating groundbreaking cases that could forever change the legal status of animals. At the AHA, I defend the bedrock principle of our democracy: the freedom of separation of church and state. The point here is that I am doing precisely what I set out to do without ever really wanting to be a lawyer because I care so deeply about the causes that I'm fighting for each and every day.

THE BOTTOM LINE: I never imagined I would become a lawyer, much less a litigator, but my passion for animal rights is what drove me to choosing this career path. If you are already sold on public interest law, my hunch is that you attended law school with public interest in mind. But many of you may not have a particular area of interest that drew you to law school. For you, an important first step is identifying a sector or cause within this umbrella to pursue. Perhaps it is broad, like environmental law or immigration law, or specific, like working for Project Innocence. It's particularly important to pursue an area you are passionate about, as the hours are long and support systems are often underwhelming at best. In short, you must balance the degree to which a cause motivates you, the relative importance of compensation, autonomy, and pride in work, and other risks and rewards that come with the non-traditional legal career.

Chapter 24

SOLOLAW

GUEST CONTRIBUTOR: **CONOR TEEVAN, SOLE PRACTITIONER (TEEVAN LAW, P.C.)**

Have you ever wondered what is really involved with setting out on your own as a sole practitioner? This enterprising lawyer did just that and describes the many benefits of a solo practice, as well as some of the unique challenges.

I know Adam through the local community here on Bainbridge Island, WA. When he asked me to contribute my perspective about having a solo law practice, I was excited to help. Having my own practice has been rewarding, satisfying, and as with any job you care about, stressful. For anyone considering this career path—whether now or in the future—I thought it would be helpful to provide a few practical tips based on my own experience.

People choose to work as sole practitioners for a lot of reasons. For me, I started my career in BigLaw and had a good experience there. But after a few years, I was pretty burned out and wanted to be more involved with working directly with clients. I took a year off and sailed to Tahiti. When that trip was over, I knew I didn't want to go back to BigLaw and would try starting my own practice.

The first thing I wanted to figure out was where my clients would come from. I expected this to be a challenge, but it ended up being easier than I excepted. There's a lot of technology out there now that connects attorneys with clients. I used platforms like UpCounsel, a website where clients post jobs, and online network groups like Select Counsel, where former BigLaw attorneys share referrals. Initially, I worked with anyone who wanted to be a client, which was its own adventure. It took maybe three years to get to the point where I had a sustainable client base. I'm now at the point where I have clients that I really care about and have real relationships with. The unexpected part for me is that I got here without doing any real marketing or networking, but I recognize that other solo practitioners have had different experiences.

Another area people ask me about is the admin and overhead time spent setting up and managing a practice. I had to figure out malpractice insurance, setting up a website, sourcing reference materials, creating a brand, pricing, and managing payroll, accounting, and taxes. This wasn't as time consuming or expensive as I expected, but it was (and is) annoying, particularly when I'm busy actually practicing law. I'm sure it varies practice to practice, but I'd say in the early years I spent under $1,000 per month on overhead. I started as a virtual practice, so those numbers don't include rent or admin support costs, and I know a lot of people do start with those costs. When calculating how much you need to start your own practice, in my opinion it's really about how much you need to support your personal lifestyle and less about covering your business overhead, as those expenses, for me, were pretty light.

I do corporate work, with a particular focus on tech start-ups. My practice covers the full life cycle of a business. Clients come to me excited and nervous to start their business, and I watch them grow, struggle, succeed, raise money, and become sustainable or get acquired, or sometimes, fold. It means a lot to me to be a part of their journey and to help them go after something they care deeply about.

This puts me in the position to help clients with all sorts of interesting challenges. We vet business ideas together and try to figure out all legal challenges that their company may face. Still, a big part of my role also involves standard legal issues, such as allocating equity or advising on employment issues or contracts with vendors or how to raise money. As I am wholly responsible for the legal services I provide, it means I spend my time doing both "partner-level" work and "assistant-level" work, and the "assistant-level" stuff can get tedious.

In terms of hours, that was one of the main draws to opening my own shop. I wanted complete control. I take days off when things are slow and work hard when needed. The flexibility allows me to travel frequently with my family, particularly for three-day weekends. But there are times when a bunch of clients all need something at the same time and there is no one I can turn to for help. Generally, I try to work from 8 a.m. to 5:30 p.m., and not on the weekends. Part of that [setup] is I've tried to position myself as a firm that provides BigLaw-quality work product at affordable pricing, but the trade-off is clients need to be a little more flexible on timing. Still, my hours end up being all over the map and it remains a challenge to figure out what works. Setting boundaries is always tough.

Work–life balance has been positive for the most part. With some notable exceptions, I am generally able to control my schedule, and I get to spend a lot of time with my family. During the week, I usually have breakfast and lunch with my kids and we almost always have dinner as a family. But as my practice has grown, I'm beginning to see real challenges. Managing ten or fifteen different clients at any given time requires thoughtful planning, setting expectations carefully, and sometimes busting your tail. My family tried to take a three-week vacation this year, but I ended up working a good chunk of it because things came up and there was no one to cover for me.

As for compensation, unlike at a firm where you have a set salary, the amount you make as a solo practitioner is directly tied to how much you work. At first, when you start growing your firm, that's a real positive. You just want to work more and make more. And you really get to see that happen, which is cool. For me, the first year was about taking whatever work came my way, but then each year was better than the year before. At some point, the trade-off between making money and working harder becomes really apparent, and you need to start thinking about what matters to you. Partners at a busy law firm earn off their associates. For me, the only way to make more is to charge more and work harder.

Outside of the relationships I've formed with clients, what I personally have found the most rewarding about having my own practice is the lifestyle. I am able to develop and maintain relationships directly with clients I care about and work with them on a schedule suitable for both of us. Last year, just before the COVID-19 pandemic hit, my family spent a month on a road trip through Baja, Mexico and I worked remotely. My clients had no problem with this, and it was an amazing adventure for my family.

The biggest challenge I've had is managing workflow. When things slow down, there's always that concern that things won't pick up again (even though they always have!), and when things pick up, all you want is for them to slow down again. The tough part is figuring out a way to manage that inconsistency. While this is something I am still trying to figure out, the good news is that there are resources out there to help. For example, I'm looking into incorporating attorney staffing groups so I can onboard help as needed. I'm also exploring more creative pricing structures that can account for some of those ebbs and flows. Having my own practice gives me the freedom to experiment with solutions.

THE BOTTOM LINE: Overall, I've enjoyed having my own practice, and I truly cannot picture re-joining a mid-sized or large firm again. The relationships I've developed with my clients, the control I have over my life, and the flexibility to work on my terms are invaluable to me. There are also real challenges that I'm still trying to figure out, particularly around managing workflow, how to expand while maintaining quality work, and feeling a part of a larger legal community. But as with everything solo shop, that's just part of the adventure.

Chapter 25

ENTREPRENEUR / JD-MBA PERSPECTIVE

GUEST CONTRIBUTOR: **SUNEEL GUPTA (FOUNDER OF RISE; AUTHOR OF *BACKABLE*)**

A former Northwestern Law classmate of mine describes his path after graduating with a JD-MBA: from founding (and selling) a start-up, to writing and publishing a book, and even running for Congress. In considering life after law school, this thought-provoking contribution asks you to reflect on whether you need to keep holding on to the things that have gotten you to this point in law (and life), or if it's time to simply let them go as you explore new horizons and the next chapter of your own story.

My name is Suneel Gupta and I graduated from Northwestern Law with a JD-MBA the same year that Adam graduated law school. We've kept in touch loosely over the years, from my days at Groupon after graduating from law school, to founding my own health care start-up (called Rise), to running for Congress, and most recently, writing a book called *Backable: The Surprising Truth Behind What Makes People Take a Chance on You*. Adam asked me to help provide insight about career options post-law school based on these experiences. While many of the key big picture concepts are covered in *Backable*, I also felt compelled to offer a few thoughts and insights that law students and legal professionals might not be able to easily find anywhere else.

I ended up in law school like many others do—at a point in which life felt directionless. I was working in an IT job in Detroit, Michigan with decent pay but mind-numbing work. Once you're in law school, I found that it can be very easy to just follow the crowd and do what everyone else is doing. At Northwestern, for many that meant interviewing for associate positions at large law firms. And I did start down that path myself, even landing an offer to join a corporate firm based in Midtown Manhattan that promised to pay more than I had ever made. But I didn't take the offer.

What did I do instead? I listened to my gut, and followed my passion. For me, that meant cold-calling people in Silicon Valley where I eventually landed at the company behind the popular Firefox web browser. I then moved on to a small start-up in Chicago that would later become Groupon, as its first head of product development. From these experiences, I learned that what I really wanted to do was start my *own* company. In fact, that's what I had wanted to do all along. While fear had initially prevented me from making that leap, I finally overcame it.

I started a company called Rise, which offered one-on-one nutrition coaching over your mobile phone. In the early days I would stand outside of Weight Watchers meetings by myself to try to recruit people to give my product a shot. Years later, Apple would name Rise the Best New App of the Year. I went on to sell the company for a decent profit to a larger company called One Medical. It wasn't the type of lucrative exit most start-up founders dream of, but it was enough to have investors give me a chance at another start-up.

But instead of taking that check, I decided to move back to my hometown in Michigan and run for Congress. This was shortly after the 2016 presidential election and I felt like I wanted to help change the direction that we seemed to be heading in. I didn't win that election.

In fact, I've undoubtedly had more failure than success in my career. But it was in those failures that I learned the most. Bill Gates once said that "success is a lousy teacher." I agree with that. But this isn't about me telling you to go out and fail, or to recycle the stale advice to "take more risks" in life. It's about feeling free to work on projects that make you come alive, even if there's a chance you may not reach the intended destination. Let me explain.

I recently joined the faculty at Harvard University and published a book called *Backable* which is all about how to convince people to take a chance on you. Whether it's starting a company, writing a book of your own, or being a great litigator, negotiator, or deal maker, the key is tapping into that inner conviction, which will ultimately lead to a rewarding career in which you find true meaning. It all starts with you. You are the one who needs to get out and inspire people to see in you what you see in yourself.

On election night in 2020, as the results were still being counted in most states, I was sharing my new book with a classroom of law students at the University of Pennsylvania. The lecture was over Zoom, and in the middle of the talk, my second grader kicked in the door to my office—just to say hello. We were eight months into the pandemic, and I was used to this. The students got a good laugh, but as Sammy was about to leave the room, I thought of something she could share with the class. Every morning since Sammy was in kindergarten, we've done a little Q&A routine on our way to school.

"What's the meaning of life?" I'll ask her. "To find your gift," she'll quickly reply.

"And what's the purpose of life?" "To give it away," she says earnestly.

Sometimes she answers energetically, but more often with an eye-roll from being asked this for the "gabajillionth" time. But she's got it down pat. When my father was around my age, he had open-heart surgery and nearly died. I always think that if something like that were to happen to me, then at least she knows the answers to those two questions.

When we shared our little routine for the class, the reaction was a bit of delight... followed by confusion. Then came an avalanche of questions. How do I know my gift? Is my gift the same as my career? Finally, one courageous student asked, "What if my gift isn't actually to be a lawyer?"

The idea that your past doesn't determine your future is hard to get your head around, even if you don't appreciate your personal history. Recovering addicts work relentlessly to break the chains of the past. But what happens when you look down from your climb with a sense of accomplishment? What will happen in five years when some of those students realize that they have a JD from a great law school, but they no longer want to practice law?

Past accomplishments and past addictions both have the power to hold us in place.

A couple of years ago I attended my own ten-year reunion at Northwestern University's School of Law. What I saw was so cliché that it's hardly worth writing about. So, let me just say this—I called my wife after the first night and shared three words: "Everyone seems miserable."

That was an exaggeration. Many of my classmates probably enjoyed their work. They were working as attorneys because they felt it actually was their Dharma. It did light their flame. But it was painfully clear that there were many other people who were practicing law only because they had a law degree. This achievement from the past seemed to almost shackle their future.

Buddha once told his disciples the story of a man who needed to cross a dangerous river. So, he spent days building a robust raft that could make it across the currents. When the man finally reached the other side, Buddha asked, did he put the heavy raft on his head and carry it for the rest of the journey?

Of course not, the disciples responded. The man left the raft behind.

So many of us are still carrying a heavy life raft on our heads. These rafts sometimes represent wonderful accomplishments that served us well in the past: an advanced degree, a high-powered job, perhaps even an important relationship. At the time we built the raft, it was exactly what we needed in our life. But it doesn't serve where we want to go from here. Ask yourself: Are you carrying any rafts that you're ready to put down?

THE BOTTOM LINE: If I could give you one piece of advice, it would be this: learn when it's time to let go of the raft. Learn to recognize when something is no longer serving you, and allow yourself to go through the sometimes painful process of letting it go. Because life is full of change—the world changes, your goals change, and you change. What you want in law school may not necessarily be what you want in ten years. And that's okay. Your past influences your future, it informs your future—but it never *determines* your future.

Part VII

LIFE AFTER LAW

As so eloquently suggested by guest contributor Suneel Gupta in the previous chapter, if your heart is ever telling you that what you love is no longer practicing law, then it's probably time to find something else to do for a profession. And if you haven't gone to law school yet, you can avoid this whole situation entirely by starting your career in an area that you have a true passion for versus something that you (or someone else) thinks you "should" or "could" do. Life really is too short to simply settle for what may be comfortable or easy, but is unsatisfying, unfulfilling, or boring.

Don't be afraid to dream of what you want to become, and don't hold yourself back by telling yourself stories of what's "realistic." You'll become your own worst enemy by undercutting the power of your conviction—and ultimately your belief in yourself—which is precisely the thing that motivates others to believe in you. To quote again from Suneel Gupta's *Backable*: "In order to succeed, you need to get out and inspire people to see in you what you see in yourself."[42]

THE BOTTOM LINE: Life after law looks different for everyone who chooses to follow this path. The key is to visualize exactly what it is that you want, and then take concrete steps to make it materialize. For example, if you want to enter a new field, start by enrolling in an online class or perhaps going to a conference where you can connect with others in that industry. This whole book started with just a single article that I posted on LinkedIn years ago. While it might take some time (and it probably will), just decide where you want to go and start taking steps in that direction. Believe in yourself and you will get there.

CLOSING REFLECTIONS

I am confident that the recognition of the importance of well-being within the legal world is increasingly inevitable. We owe it to ourselves to have these important conversations about the things that matter most, even if it's hard. I see this guide as one small piece of that larger and very significant evolution in the field of law. My goal is to elevate the focus on well-being in all areas of the profession by empowering you to make choices I wish I had made earlier myself.

As Deepak Chopra says: "In every moment, you have a choice about how you want to use two of your most precious resources: your attention, and your intention."[43] As this guide comes to a close, I hope that making conscious choices, using both your attention and intention, comes more easily to you from this moment onwards. While much of the guidance covered here has been through the lens of the legal profession, you've probably come to realize it's applicable to anyone seeking positive change. By increasing your awareness and being more mindful of your choices, you truly *can* change your life. Always remember it is *your* life and *your* choices.

THE BOTTOM LINE: In the midst of a global pandemic, and in a world that somehow manages to feel more turbulent and uncertain than ever before, I truly hope that the tools and advice in this guide will help you to find calmness, clarity, and stability as you take on life in law school and beyond. Here's to **surthriving** in all of your adventures.

"My mission in life is not merely to survive, but to thrive; and to do so with some passion, some compassion, some humor and some style."

—MAYA ANGELOU[44]

APPENDIX

TO GO OR NOT TO GO TO LAW SCHOOL, THAT IS THE QUESTION...

Every lawyer I know has a pretty strong opinion when asked by an aspiring law student the age-old question: "Should I go to law school?" This guide wouldn't be complete without offering my own candid thoughts on that momentous decision. For what it's worth, I always used to say: "No matter what, don't go. It's a terrible waste of money that you'll inevitably regret. Seriously, save yourself." My response now is the much more nuanced question: "What do you want to do?"

Here's the thing. When you ask most lawyers about going to law school, they tend to answer based on what *their* experience has been versus relating it to what *you* want in life. This is where my question comes in. As you have read in this guide, there are usually many different paths to satisfy a given career goal. And if you're not exactly sure *what* you want to do, it's probably worth figuring out the answer *before* choosing a path that potentially involves massive amounts of student debt (see "Keeping costs in mind" on page 263 for more on that point).

FIND YOUR PURPOSE

I believe the key is to approach the question about whether to attend law school from your **purpose and/or passion** versus just something you think might eventually get you closer to your goal (or just more money than you're making now). Merely being interested in a topic, industry, or field (whether it's technology, the environment, or banking) does not mean you will actually enjoy practicing law in that particular area. At all.

When someone tells me they are interested in a given field, it always prompts me to ask: "What is it about that type of law that specifically interests you?" Or sometimes I just ask again: "But what do you actually *want* to do?" Because if the answer is something along the lines of "I want to be involved in the [fill in the blank] industry," then getting a law degree isn't necessarily the right career choice. While you may have strong interest in a particular topic, you need to have better clarity in what you actually want to do in life.

Let's say your dream job is working in show business. If what you're picturing is working with movie stars or being part of the creative process, then going to law school is unlikely to help. Why? You could wind up taking a job as an entertainment lawyer where much of your day is spent drafting and revising agreements—albeit agreements for films and/or television shows. A better choice might be skipping law school altogether (at least for now) and getting a job that doesn't require a legal degree, but one that does involve much more exposure to the creative process. That way, you won't have committed to the potentially overwhelming costs of law school only to find out that being a lawyer is not actually your desired career path. If things don't work out, going to law school will still always be an option for you down the road.

If you think your true calling is standing before a jury making a closing argument in a major trial, or drafting a brief that gets filed with the Supreme Court of the United States, then of course going to law school is a necessity. But if you're not quite sure what you want to do with your law degree, then it's important to consider whether there is a more direct way to do something you'll love for your livelihood. Ask yourself if there are other job options that could be just as satisfying or impactful. What about working in politics for a candidate who wants to change the immigration laws, working for a think tank, or doing research at a university? The possibilities are endless!

Further thoughts: *As stated in his article, "Free Yourself from What You Should Be Doing," author Andy Molinsky has these wise words to consider:*

"But when your compliance system systematically overrides your personal passion, that's when it's critical to examine on a broader level whether you're living the life you want to lead. [...] And by identifying and escaping your compliant zone

[a sense of what you 'should' but may not want to pursue, e.g., in ways expected by your parents, your extended family, or your culture], you can discover your 'true' self—the part of you that reflects your authentic passions and interests and leads to a more fulfilling life."[45]

For anyone out there who still isn't quite sure what your "why" is yet, try using the Finding Your "Why" worksheet in the Additional Resources section.

TRY BEFORE YOU BUY

The unfortunate reality is that the actual practice of law is simply not that fulfilling for many legal professionals (just look at some of the statistics and stories).[46] If you're not sure what being a lawyer is actually like, then I highly recommend taking a year or two to work at a law firm or with lawyers in some capacity before going to law school. This will give you a behind-the-scenes look at the actual work they are doing. You should also talk to as many practicing lawyers as you can, read what the guest contributors in this guide have shared, and find mentors to advise you.

As an undergrad, I worked as a file clerk for a mid-sized firm in Los Angeles, and did a brief stint for a sole practitioner, which is a law practice run by a single lawyer.

I also worked at an internet start-up with many burned out ex-lawyers who helped design online compliance training courses. In addition to some much-needed spending money, these jobs gave me an invaluable opportunity to see, hear, and speak to lawyers about their jobs on a regular basis.

One of the biggest takeaways for me was how many of the lawyers who went straight from college to law school wished that they had taken some time off in between to explore other interests. And pretty much everyone who *had* taken time off to pursue other interests said they were glad they did, even if they ultimately ended up going to law school like I did.

I used my time off before law school to try everything, from working in the California legislature and on a presidential campaign in Iowa, to starting a business. I even worked at a local pub on nights and weekends. By exploring these other options, I felt more confident that applying to law school was the right career choice for me, and I wasn't left wondering how those other career paths might have turned out. When it came time to interviewing for positions after law school, these extra years of experience also came in handy. If there is anything that you might want to do more than or equally as much as law, the time to go for it is before committing to law school.

THE ACTUAL PRACTICE OF LAW

My experience working at one of the largest and most prestigious law firms in New York City was that much of the work is incredibly unfulfilling at best, and soul crushing at worst. Like me, many (if not most) junior attorneys at large law firms start their legal careers reviewing massive amounts of documents, either doing "doc review" as litigation associates or "due diligence" on the corporate side. Regardless of what it's called, for most people, it's not particularly enjoyable (especially when you're doing it at midnight!), let alone rewarding from a career perspective since it usually means sitting in front of a computer screen reviewing hundreds of documents a day. Even when I progressed to more interesting and engaging work assignments, there was often still very little interaction with anyone, aside from more senior attorneys asking for status updates and assigning me more work. The pressure to bill hours is also always present, which can make it difficult to prioritize even basic personal wants and needs outside of work, which was the case for me. Even so-called "lifestyle firms" are dependent on billable hours to keep the lights on.

It's certainly not all bad. For example, the documents that you're reviewing can be extremely important in a litigation. It was also interesting to learn about the client's business and industry through doing doc review. Of course, the biggest perk is the pay. Current salaries for first-year associates at large law firms are an astronomical $190,000.[47]

Just having the opportunity to do this type of work, for this amount of money, carries a huge amount of privilege and opportunity that is foreclosed to many law school graduates (or most people, for that matter). I also have many good friends and mentors who still practice law at law firms, from small ones they started to BigLaw, and greatly enjoy what they do for a living. And I learned a ton during my years at large law firms—it ultimately just wasn't the right long-term fit for me on my career journey.

Important note: *There are many other types of legal careers that do not involve large law firms (see the "Beyond BigLaw" guest contributions in Part VI for additional perspectives on some of those possible career paths). But due to the enormous cost of attending law school, many graduates find themselves in a position like I did—pursuing jobs that they hadn't planned on in order to repay their student loans.*

At the end of the day, even if you are fortunate to land a high-paying BigLaw job, you have to ask yourself what is the point of making exceptional amounts of money if you are spending almost all of your waking moments—including nights and weekends—at work, reviewing documents. If you're a "people person" like I am, spending day after day devoid of any meaningful human interaction can quickly become problematic from a mental health and well-being perspective.

KEEPING COSTS IN MIND

If you do decide to go to law school, please remember that you don't have to choose a school that requires taking out huge loans to attend, and you don't have to accept every loan that's offered to you. Strongly consider attending schools which offer a scholarship or that have lower overall costs of attendance. Keep in mind that the more debt you graduate with, the less flexibility you will have in choosing a job. Moreover, there is **absolutely no guarantee** that taking on large amounts of student loan debt to attend law school will result in being able to secure a high-paying job that will allow you to actually repay those big loans. To the contrary, many law school graduates unfortunately find themselves in much lower-paying jobs than they had anticipated. This can have significant negative impact on both financial and mental well-being, including delaying saving for retirement or emergencies, having the ability to make a down payment and/or mortgage payments, or constrained lifestyle choices (e.g., where to live, travel, and/or vacation).

For all of these reasons, it is extremely important to fully evaluate all of the potential risks—along with potential benefits—when making your decision of which law school to attend. It could very well be that things like a global alumni network, strong international programs, the overall campus vibe/aesthetic/environment and strong sense of community outweigh the potential financial downside. Just be very aware and intentional about your decision.

THE BOTTOM LINE: Often the people you approach for a conversation about whether to go or not to go to law school have a goal to talk someone either out of or into making one of the most significant decisions of their lives. I've had this conversation with a lot of people and this is my general advice: Figure out what it is you actually want to do first, then figure out if law school will help you accomplish that goal, or if there might be another path that is more directly tied to what you truly want and enjoy in life. No matter what, make sure to use the tools outlined in Part I of this guide as a foundation for whatever lies ahead.

NOTES

1. Definitions taken from dictionary.com.
2. The Surthriving Law website is located at https://www.surthrivinglaw.com.
3. Jeremy Adam Smith, Kira M. Newman, Jill Suttie and Hooria Jazaieri, "The State of Mindfulness Science," *Greater Good* magazine, December 5, 2017, https://greatergood.berkeley.edu/article/item/ the_state_of_mindfulness_science.
4. Women's National Basketball Association, "Headspace, NBA and WNBA Launch Co-Branded Performance Mindset Category Within Meditation and Mindfulness App," June 12, 2019, https://www.wnba.com/news/headspace-nba-and-wnba-launch-co-branded-performance-mindset-category-within-meditation-and-mindfulness-app/.
5. Sean Grabowski, "Celebrities and Athletes Who Meditate Every Day," March 1, 2020, https://themindfulsteward.com/celebrities-and-athletes-who-meditate-everyday/.
6. Our family's favorite *Sesame Street* Monster Meditation is "Goodnight Body with Elmo." "*Sesame Street* Monster Meditation #2: Goodnight Body with Elmo and Headspace," YouTube video, 3:08, "Sesame Street," April 29, 2020, https://www.youtube.com/watch?v=yhRWp0wOLyo.
7. Readers may want to check out short meditation exercises such as the sixteen-second "pattern interrupt" meditation with davidji. "16 Second Technique to Master Your Emotions

with davidji," YouTube video, 2:08, "Hay House," July 30, 2015, https://www.youtube.com/watch?v=-G_MhMzwunA.

8. For current pricing for You Need A Budget, please see their website. YouNeedABudget.com, https://www.youneedabudget.com/pricing.
9. Read more about the four rules on the YNAB website.
10. Katy Milkman, *How to Change: The Science of Getting from Where You Are to Where You Want to Be*. New York, NY: Portfolio/Penguin, 2021, pp. 43-49.
11. James Clear, *Atomic Habits: An Easy & Proven Way to Build Good Habits & Break Bad Ones*. New York, NY: Penguin Publishing Group, 2018, p. 41.
12. Peter M. Gollwitzer, "Implementation intentions: Strong effects of simple plans," *American Psychologist*, no. 54, pp. 490–503. https://doi.org/10.1037/0003-066X.54.7.493.
13. Deepak Chopra, as heard in "Getting Unstuck: Creating a Limitless Life," a 21-Day Meditation Experience with Oprah and Deepak, accessed at https://chopracentermeditation.com.
14. Clear, *Atomic Habits*, p. 67.
15. Clear, *Atomic Habits*, p. 62.
16. As quoted in the Productivity Planner by Intelligent Change, p. 9.
17. Check out the BestSelf's Self Journal on their website: https://bestself.co/products/self-journal.
18. Cathryn Lavery, as quoted on page 3 of "Quick Start Guide" of the Self Journal Guidebook, BestSelf Ventures, LLC, 2020.
19. Amy Morin, "7 Scientifically Proven Benefits of Gratitude That Will Motivate You To Give Thanks Year-Round," *Forbes*

magazine, November 23, 2014, https://www.forbes.com/sites/amymorin/2014/11/23/7-scientifically-proven-benefits-of-gratitude-that-will-motivate-you-to-give-thanks-year-round/?sh=2a5cfb2d183c.

20. You can find the 30-Day Gratitude Journal here: https://bestself.co/products/30-day-gratitude-journal.
21. "One study, which examined data from more than 309,000 people, found that lack of strong relationships increased the risk of premature death from all causes by 50%—an effect on mortality risk roughly comparable to smoking up to 15 cigarettes a day, and greater than obesity and physical inactivity." Harvard Women's Health Watch, "The Health Benefits of Strong Relationships," Harvard Health Publishing, Harvard Medical School, first published August 6, 2019; updated December, 2010, https://www.health.harvard.edu/newsletter_article/the-health-benefits-of-strong-relationships. See also Stephen J. Bronner, "3 Psychological Benefits of a *Collaborative* Professional Network," *Inverse* magazine, February 11, 2020, https://www.inverse.com/mind-body/psychological-benefits-of-networking.
22. I highly recommend *Mindful Listening* by Harvard Business Review from the HBR Emotional Intelligence Series, published by Harvard Business Publishing.
23. LinkedIn mission statement, LinkedIn, https://about.linkedin.com.
24. Find out more on the SEO Scholar program here: https://www.seo-usa.org/scholars/.
25. Abraham H. Maslow, *Toward a Psychology of Being*. U.S.: John Wiley & Sons, Inc., 3rd edition, 1998 [Kindle].

26. Catherine Moore, "What is Eudaimonia? Aristotle and Eudaimonic Well-Being," PositivePsychology.com, May 3, 2021, https://positivepsychology.com/eudaimonia/.
27. Matthew J. Van Natta, *The Beginner's Guide To Stoicism: Tools for Emotional Resilience and Positivity*. Althea Press, 2019, pp. 47-48.
28. Van Natta, *The Beginner's Guide To Stoicism*, p. 60.
29. Van Natta, *The Beginner's Guide To Stoicism*, p. 48.
30. Check out the LEEWS method at: https://leews.com/.
31. Read my note here: "Business Implications of Divergences in Multi-Jurisdictional Merger Review by International Competition Enforcement Agencies," *Northwestern Journal of International Law and Business*, vol. 28, issue 1, pp.147–170, https://scholarlycommons.law.northwestern.edu/njilb/vol28/iss1/7/.
32. Mary Abbajay, "Mentoring Matters: Three Essential Elements of Success," *Forbes* magazine, January 20, 2019, https://www.forbes.com/sites/maryabbajay/2019/01/20/mentoring-matters-three-essential-element-of-success/?sh=5b5607e145a9.
33. University of Oxford, "Happy Workers are 13% More Productive," October 24, 2019, https://www.ox.ac.uk/news/2019-10-24-happy-workers-are-13-more-productive.
34. Virgina Sharma, as posted on LinkedIn, April 30, 2021, https://www.linkedin.com/posts/virginiasharma_mentalhealth-activity-6794304870099775488-w93k.
35. Elizabeth Deeley, quoted in "Kirkland's Hunt for Roughly 245 Summer Associates in U.S.," as reported by Casey Sullivan, Bloomberg Law, August 4, 2017, https://news.bloomberglaw.

com/business-and-practice/kirklands-hunt-for-roughly-245-summer-associates-in-u-s/.

36. Here are two articles describing research studies on bias in interviewing:

    i. Iris Bohnet, "How to Take the Bias out of Interviews," *Harvard Business Review*, April 18, 2018, https://hbr org/2016/04/how-to-take-the-bias-out-of-interviews.

    ii. Sarah Laskow, "Want the best person for the job? Don't interview," *Boston Globe*, November 24, 2013, https://www.bostonglobe.com/ideas/2013/11/24/want best-person-for-job-don-interview/3LB4rwjf6i88GfaDoRub LN/story.html.

37. Jason Kanner, as quoted in "Kirkland's Hunt for Roughly 245 Summer Associates in U.S."
38. Amy Gallo, "How to Nail a Job Interview—Remotely," *Harvard Business Review*, June 22, 2020, https://hbr.org/2020/06/how-to-nail-a-job-interview-remotely.
39. Suneel Gupta and Carlye Alder, *Backable: The Surprising Truth Behind What Makes People Take A Chance On You*, New York, NY: Little, Brown, and Company, 2021, p.17.
40. Cassandra Sanford, as quoted on page 4 of "Quick Start Guide" of the Self Journal Guidebook, BestSelf Ventures, LLC, 2020.
41. Find out more about the BBS Fellowship here: https://bradleybernsteinllp.com/fellowship.html.
42. Gupta, *Backable*, p. 14.
43. Deepak Chopra, as heard in "Getting Unstuck: Creating a Limitless Life."

44. Maya Angelou, Facebook post, July 4, 2011, https://www.facebook.com/MayaAngelou/posts/10150251846629796.
45. Andy Molinsky, "Free Yourself from What You 'Should' Be Doing," *Harvard Business Review*, January 18, 2017, https://hbr.org/2017/01/free-yourself-from-what-you-should-be-doing.
46. Stephen Carter, "Why Lawyers are Miserable," *The Chicago Tribune*, September 7, 2015, https://www.chicagotribune.com/opinion/commentary/ct-why-lawyers-are-miserable-20150907-story.html.
47. See more salary information in the National Association for Law Placement's (NALP) new 2019 Associate Salary Survey at https://www.nalp.org/0619research.
48. Amir Moini, *22 Life Lessons By Someone More F*cked Up Than You*, U.S., 2020, p.121.
49. Moini, *22 Life Lessons*, p.105.

ACKNOWLEDGMENTS

To Alexis for being such an amazing and dedicated partner. You truly changed my life for the (much) better. Thank goodness for the one open seat next to you at law school orientation!

To my kids for bringing me such great joy and for inspiring me to actually finish this project.

To Mom for always believing in me and for being my biggest champion.

To Dad, Reba, Ryan, Andrew, and Hannah for the bottomless love, acceptance, and support.

To Jane and Guy for making me feel like I've always been part of the family.

To the many friends and other family members for taking my calls and texts, and hearing way more about this whole adventure than they ever asked to (or probably wanted).

To the guest contributors for their selfless dedication, and for somehow finding the time to provide such impactful and important advice and insight. I am forever grateful for your contributions.

To all of the law students who took valuable time to provide such candid and actionable feedback (including the idea of adding guest contributors in the first place).

To Kyle Sommer for believing in this project and for all of his helpful input and introductions.

To my former law school advisor Bill Chamberlain for his "tough love" notes on an early draft of the manuscript and helping me make (many) changes for the better.

To my copy editor Maddy Curry for all of the great catches and to Sarah Beaudin for introducing us (not to mention the stellar interior design and layout work).

To Adam Renvoize for his exceptional patience in bringing my vision for the cover design to life.

To Dr. Arnie for introducing me to the survive, stabilize, and thrive framework.

And finally to Darryl O'Daniel, for providing hope when I needed it most.

ADDITIONAL RESOURCES

Visit the Surthriving Law website to download free digital versions of all materials referenced in this section.

FINDING YOUR "WHY" WORKSHEET

Having a plan or road map (with built-in flexibility and contingencies) is crucial for career success and personal happiness. One astute mentor provided me with the following helpful feedback: "I encourage prospective law students to do some soul searching and identify their purpose and their 'why,' and map out their areas of interest/expertise (as I did with my career coach after law school) to help identify the best fit for law school and area of law to practice. Charting their law school/career path in this way saves much time and expense, avoids stress (and that quarter-life crisis five years after law school!), and helps them find a career that they truly enjoy."

As guest contributor Alison Maxell nicely summed it up: "The bottom line is that each of us only gets to pass this way once. Do it right. Be true to yourself and your passions. And above all else, believe in yourself. If you do these things, then success, as you define it, is pretty much guaranteed." Another guest contributor noted in Chapter 22: "[I] certainly could have benefited by a little more focus on my larger career goals and how my day-to-day choices were helping (or harming) my ability to reach them." And as entrepreneur and author Suneel Gupta so touchingly shared in his daily exchange with his daughter: "What is the meaning of life? To find your gift. And what's the purpose of life? To give it away." This worksheet helps you reflect on your own answers to these questions.

Reflection #1

What is your gift, your superpower, your dharma—i.e., the one most exceptional thing about yourself that you can share with the world? For example, mine is the ability to connect with others and help them discover their true purpose.

____

____

____

____

Reflection #2

What are three things that you love to do most in life? *(e.g., spend time with my family, travel, sports)*

#1	#2	#3

Reflection #3

Which career path(s) might most directly help you incorporate these things into your life?

____

____

Reflection #4

Who can you seek out for advice on each of your ideas on potential career paths listed in the previous reflection?

____

____

*Suggested reading: *The Why Café* by John P. Strelecky

LINKEDIN MESSAGING EXAMPLES

As discussed throughout this guide, sending messages via LinkedIn is an effective way to make new connections and build your professional network—before, during, and after law school. I went back to my own archives in order to provide you with some examples of ways to approach using LinkedIn for your own networking. Remember to always tailor messages that you send so that they are in your own voice and style, gracious, specific, and actionable.

The following are two examples of strong inbound LinkedIn messages I have received in the past twelve months. The content and specificity of each message encouraged me to respond and engage with each of these individuals.

EXAMPLE 1: CURRENT LAW STUDENT

Dear Adam,

Firstly, I'd like to thank you for sharing your insights and advice for law students. As a fellow Bruin [...], I was really glad to find your article on OCI strategies last summer after my first year at [firm name].

Honestly, I don't think I would be able to network and prepare for interviews successfully if I hadn't found your article. I managed to get a full-time offer from [firm name], despite having a less-than-stellar GPA.

I couldn't help but reach out to you as a rising 3L because I'm also very interested in privacy/cybersecurity law and plan to participate in the 3L OCI again, as you did—while I got a return offer from [firm name], the firm canceled its summer program entirely due to the COVID pandemic.

While I want to pursue a career in privacy and tech law, I understand firms hiring 3Ls mostly look for candidates interested in specific practice areas—corporate, bankruptcy, etc. Because I'm looking for BigLaw jobs as a 3L, I'm not sure whether I should strategize to be hired in practice areas that are likely to be busy during the recession—i.e., restructuring, bankruptcy, corporate finance—instead of privacy/tech law?

I don't have any prior work experience in tech/cybersecurity but have taken a couple of courses in [subject]. I also have [multiple positions lined up] for this summer: [describes positions]. Also, during this summer, I plan to be certified in [program]. Would you recommend this?

I sincerely appreciate your help and advice. Have a great day!

Best,
2L

EXAMPLE 2: LEGAL PROFESSIONAL

Hey Adam: How are you? It looks like my path is tracking in the same direction as yours. I left my company for a bit but came back recently to focus on compliance. I have a friend who's looking at a director role where you work and I thought of you and your role. I was wondering if you'd be willing to chat with him to the extent that you interact with that position. Thanks, and hope all is well.

Finally, here are two examples of (short and sweet) personalized messages that I've used when inviting others to connect with me via LinkedIn.

> Hi [NAME]: Just saw your message to the [networking group] and thought it would be great to connect with you directly here via LinkedIn as well! Really impressed with how your professional profile is presented btw! All the best, Adam

> Really great connecting with you @ [event] this morning, [name]. Would be great to also connect with you here on LinkedIn. Hope the trips to Singapore & Nairobi go well!
> Best, Adam

NETWORKING EMAIL EXAMPLES

While there are always new apps and ways of communicating (such as TikTok & Clubhouse), email is still a common and important way of networking for legal professionals. As with the LinkedIn messages, I've gone back to my inbox to find actual messages used during my own job search. Here are examples of emails I sent requesting assistance and to gain further insight into firms, the interviewing process, and the hiring process while I was in law school.

Subject: Northwestern Law/D.C. Questions

Dear [Northwestern 2L Student]:

I just finished my first year at Northwestern and am currently working at the Antitrust Division of the U.S. Department of Justice in D.C. for the summer.

You're listed as one of the "peer counselors" [from Northwestern Law] for questions about working in D.C. so I thought I'd shoot you an email.

Basically, I'm interested in seeing what the [on-campus interviewing] process was like for you and if you had to do a lot of outside work (i.e., sending letters & resumes) to get an offer/position in D.C. I'll probably be interviewing in New York as well, but my background (3 years in the California Legislature doing work on public utilities) and interests (antitrust work) seem better suited for the D.C. market.

In general, it doesn't seem like too many D.C. employers come to campus, but I've heard that not many Northwestern students interview with the D.C. firms so it balances out.

I guess that's about it. Any thoughts/info/advice you have would be greatly appreciated.

Thanks for your time,
Adam

Subject: Northwestern Follow-up

Dear [Law Firm Partner]:

My name is Adam Hunt and I spoke with you for some time at Northwestern Law School's "Meet the Firm" night earlier this year. I'm working in D.C. for the summer at the U.S. Department of Justice Antitrust Division and I thought I'd follow up with you to see if there are any "open house" type events at [firm] before I leave in August. I was really hoping to see the office while I was here but didn't want to just drop by unannounced. Thanks for your time and I hope that you had a good Fourth of July!

Sincerely,
Adam Hunt

Subject: Northwestern Student Inquiry

Dear [Law Firm Partner]:

My name is Adam Hunt and I am a second-year legal student at Northwestern University living in Washington, D.C. for the summer. I understand that you are an alumnus of Northwestern and I'm writing to see if it would be possible to arrange for a brief informational interview before I return to Chicago on August 6th.

I'm particularly interested in learning more about your practice involving [subject] at [firm]. I have been working at the Transportation, Energy and Agriculture section of the DOJ's Antitrust Division this summer and am interested in continuing to work on [these types of] issues once I graduate from Northwestern.

I've attached a copy of my resume for your review and would appreciate the opportunity to respond to any questions that you might have about my previous work experience or interests.

Thank you very much for your time.

—Adam

Subject: NUSL Alumni Interviewing

Dear [Law Firm Partner]:

I'm flying into the District this Sunday (5/28) and starting my job at DOJ Antitrust on Tuesday, May 30th so the first week of June might be a good time to shoot for. I'll be working fairly close to your office and am happy to meet there whenever you are available.

As far as skills go, I'm most interested in working on interview questions I can expect to get for a summer associate position. Specifically, I'd like to work on the most difficult questions I might face in interviews for a firm job as well as those questions that may differ from typical interview questions.

Thanks for your time, I really appreciate it!
—Adam

PS: I will make sure to forward my resume to you next week once I've updated it with my summer job information.

SHARING YOUR OWN JOURNEY

A sincere hope of mine is that by sharing my personal journey, it will help create connections and discussions about the experiences of others. As you've seen from the guest contributions included in this guide, sharing your perspective can truly make a difference in the lives of others.

If you found value from this surthrival guide, I hope that you will share that with others in your network—at school, work, or elsewhere—to help increase the overall understanding and attention to well-being both in the legal community and in the broader world that we live in.

Shameless plug alert! *Leaving a review on Amazon is a particularly helpful way to bring awareness to this important work, and I would be deeply grateful for anyone who takes the time to do so—even a short and sweet note can be incredibly influential.*

To the extent that anything did not resonate, or seems contrary to your experience, it's important for me to hear that feedback as well. You can submit any thoughts through my website, or you can simply email me directly (adam@surthrivinglaw.com). I am committed to personally responding to anyone who takes the time and energy to connect with me.

I've learned there is always an opportunity to improve self-awareness and understanding. As my colleague Amir Moini recently wrote in his book *22 Life Lessons by Someone More F*cked Up Than You*, "I think it is important to realize that even with the best intentions, everyone still has a bias to some degree, including myself."[48] Moini also (correctly) notes: "I think it's important to know that if everything else in your life is good enough—you are trying to find your purpose, your passion, your happiness—you are already in a pretty good position to begin with."[49] As I look back on my own journey, experiences, and advice in this book, it is important for me to acknowledge the incredible privilege that I have had in my life, and the significant work I still have to do interrogating my own biases. I am sincerely committed to doing this work, and continuing to learn, listen, and taking action in allyship.

It honestly feels pretty scary to put something like this out into the world, but the potential opportunity to help people on their journey is part of my purpose. I hope that by actually completing my own passion project, I have inspired you to have the courage to take a bold step into the unknown, too, and to choose vulnerability over fear, and hope over doubt.

Always choose hope over doubt.

PERSONAL COMMITMENT

If you're anything like me, you can't read something like this without wanting to actually do something. In fact, the whole point of writing this guide was to help you do things differently than I did. Now that you've reached the end of this book, it's your turn. What is one specific commitment that you want to make?

Some examples of commitments include:

- To start meditating after I finish breakfast tomorrow morning.
- To make an exercise plan for this week as soon as I put this book down.
- To use LinkedIn to find connections for my summer job search.
- To start doing [insert activity you love but have put on hold] again.
- To call my grandparents at noon on Friday to tell them how much I love them.

My Commitment:

____

____

____

IN LOVING MEMORY

For my grandmother Me-m, who taught me a thing or two about surthriving, and my grandfather Papa, who was the most important lawyer in my life.

I will miss you both so much.

Northwestern Law graduation weekend. Chicago, IL (2008)

Made in the USA
Monee, IL
23 July 2024

62518226R10167